THE SILK ROAD SAGA

Jean-Pierre Drège   Emil M. Bührer

THE
SILK ROAD
SAGA

**with over 350 colour photographs
taken by the photographers
of Japanese State Television, NHK, Tokyo**

Facts On File
New York • Oxford

Library of Congress Cataloging-in-Publication Data

Drège, Jean-Pierre.
  [Route de la Soie, English]
  The Silk Road Saga / Jean-Pierre Drège
    p.   cm.
  Translation of: La Route de la Soie.
  Bibliography: p.
  ISBN 0-81602-211-9
  1. Silk Road — History. 2. Silk Road — History — Pictorial works. 3. Asia — Description and travel — 1951- 4. Asia — Description and travel — 1951- — Views. I. Title.
DS5.5.D7413   1989
915.04'428 — dc20

British Library Cataloguing in Publication Data

Drège, Jean-Pierre, 1946
  The Silk Road Saga.
  1. China. Xinjiang-Uighur Autonomous Region, history
  I. Title   II. La route de soie. *English*
951'.6
  ISBN 0-81602-211-9

General direction:
Motovun (Switzerland) Co-Publishing Comp., Ltd., Lucerne
Editor-in-chief: Nebojsa-Bato Tomasević
Cartography: Touring Club Italiano, Milan
Translation from the French by Adrian Room

© 1986 by Motovun (Switzerland) Co-Publishing Company Ltd., Lucerne and Yugoslav Review, Belgrade

© 1986 for the photographs by Nippon Hoso Kyokai and Nippon Hoso Shuppan Kyokai, Tokyo

© 1989 for the English-language edition by Facts On File Publications

Facts On File, Inc.
460 Park Avenue South
New York NY 10016
USA

Facts On File, Ltd.
Collins Street
Oxford OX4 IXJ
United Kingdom

Printed in Italy

TABLE OF CONTENTS

The Silk Road, along which passed not only merchandise but also ideas,
manufacturing techniques and religions,
was the symbol of the bond between East and West.
As we follow it here from China to Italy,
we shall discover, over a fascinating journey,
The complexity of the exchanges and variety of landscapes and cultures.

FOREWORD

The Silk Road is a comparatively recent concept. It was only towards the end of the 19th century that the geographer Ferdinand von Richthofen, describing the trading routes between China, Central Asia and the West, used the term *Seidenstrassen,* without any further explanation. Since then, the Silk Road has come to embody a collection of trading routes between China and West, and so it is a convenient term that embraces a complex reality. Today, the name has come to be equally adopted by both the West and by China and Japan.

In fact, it consists of a whole network of routes which have come to make their way across Eurasia over the centuries, adapting their function according to the political situation, economic conditions, taste and demand of different races for particular products, dissemination of religious beliefs or artistic themes, development of technology, and so on. Since the earliest times land and sea routes have coexisted. Frequently, the two types of routes are complementary, with caravans and ships travelling in succession to transport the merchandise.

Across this multiplicity of routes, silk has become the common bond between East and West, generating various myths and legends which have sometimes eclipsed the other products being transported. The route taken by silk was thus the route taken by spices, tea, paper and chinaware. Conversely, it was also the route of lucerne and the grape, of glass and incense. As well, of course, it was the route taken by Buddhism and Nestorianism.

But it is silk which, because of its sheer luxury, has come to give its name to this complex of roads and routes. And it was silk, in fact, which served as the basic currency between China and the neighbouring peoples of the North and West. It represented the tribute paid by the Chinese to their nomadic neighbours in order to ensure peace and to guard against raids and the destruction of their crops. Little by little, through the bartering of surplus supplies, silk became highly sought after in the Roman Empire.

In reality, there were two contrasting aspects to these exchanges. For the Chinese, silk was simply a product to be traded, and China expected nothing special in return from the West. Western envoys, on arriving in the Chinese capital, would bring rich and rare objects or products from their own countries, by way of homage from their sovereign and as a token of their obeisance. In return, they would be generously supplied with silken goods. Moreover, the selling of silk to the nomadic tribes was carried out by Chinese government agents, not by traders. It was only later that it became a currency and a means of exchange. Even so, under the Earlier Han dynasty (206 BC – AD 8), trade was strictly limited. On the other hand, the taste for silk fabrics which grew rapidly in the West resulted in an increased demand for it, and in the development of its trade, with the involvment of a whole host of middlemen. Dealings with China were purely connected with trade, and nothing else.

Opposite: On the caravan routes which criss-crossed the East from the Mediterranean to Northern China, the camel was the means of transport best adapted to cross the sands and deserts.

In the 10th century BC, the Emperor Mu is said to have made a journey to the West and during the course of it to have stayed with Xiwangmu, the Queen Mother of the West. According to Alfred Forke, Xiwangmu was the Queen of Sheba. But he was almost certainly mistaken. However, this particular legend, which became embroidered with strands of other legends, themselves based on reasonably certain events, gave credence to the notion of a *terra incognita* or Unknown Land. The Chinese placed this in the far western extremity of the world. Its location inevitably became closer when the limits of the known world were more clearly defined, so that the Queen Mother of the West sought refuge in the Paradise of Immortality and came to reign there.

EAST AND WEST

CHINA AND THE WESTERN WORLD

The raids made by the Xiongnu horsemen were one of the reasons behind the opening of the Silk Road: the journey of Zhang Qian to Central Asia had the original main aim of seeking an alliance against them.

The Adventures of Zhang Qian

The first real penetration made by the Chinese into the West was brought about by the problems caused by the Xiongnu, traditionally recognised as the ancestors of the Huns, to the Han empire. The troubles resulted from the conflict between two cultures: nomads and settled peoples, stock-raisers and crop-growers. And it was precisely this antagonism that resulted in the construction of the Great Wall of China.

To the Han, the Xiongnu were seen as a permanent enemy. As stock-raisers, they were also hunters and good horsemen, causing widespread ruin wherever they went before passing on their way. Raids and forays into the territory of the Chinese were incessant. Before the coming of the First Emperor, Shih Huang Ti, who in 221 BC had successfully united the kingdoms of Central China, the Xiongnu had been calm and peaceful, especially after the building of the Great Wall. But under the Han dynasty, they resumed their raids, thus flouting imperial authority. It was only under Wudi, the warrior emperor (reigned 141 – 87 BC) that the incursions of the Xiongnu were effectively stemmed. General Huo Qubing (died 117 BC) spent much of his time warring in the north-west, in the present province of Kansu.

Since the Xiongnu could not be restrained with any lasting effect, Emperor Wu decided to seek an alliance with the Yuezhi, who were enemies of the Xiongnu. Xiongnu prisoners had spoken of their experiences under the Yuezhi, who, like them, were a nomadic people. They lived in the region of Dunhuang and the Qilian Mountains, where they had been defeated and expelled by the Xiongnu. As was the custom, the *shanyu* (king of the Yuezhi), on killing their king, had made a drinking bowl from his skull. The Yuezhi had fled westwards, to the Ili valley, from where they were again expelled by the Wusun, another nomadic race, believed to be the *Asmiraioi* mentioned by Ptolemy. They then seem to have settled in Sogdiana, in the region of Samarkand, and after that in Bactra (later known as Balkh) having in their turn driven out its own people. It was the Yuezhi who subsequently founded the Indoscythian empire of the Kushan (1st – 3rd centuries) in the north of India. In the Chinese capital, it was thought that the Yuezhi must have developed a deep resentment for the Xiongnu. But the emperor knew for certain that they had settled in a remote territory and he resolved to send them an emissary. The man he chose for this mission was a court functionary, Zhang Qian. To reach the Yuezhi, he would have to cross Xiongnu territory. Inevitably, no sooner had he left China than he was captured. He remained a prisoner for ten years, during which time he married a nomad wife who bore him children.

Still mindful of his original mission, Zhang Qian one day seized his chance and escaped with his companions, continuing his journey westwards in search of the Yuezhi. He came first to Dayuan (Ferghana Valley), where the king made him welcome. Then he arrived in Kangju (a region of Samarkand), and so finally to the Yuezhi. Once there, however, he discovered to his surprise that the Yuezhi were living in peace and contentment without any intention of taking their revenge on the Xiongnu. After staying a year in Bactra without succeeding in interesting the Yuezhi in fighting the Xiongnu, Zhang Qian thus set off on the return journey. He was once again captured by the Xiongnu, but this time was held for only a year. In the confusion that followed the death of the king, Zhang Qian, together with his wife and guide, managed to escape. He was well received by the emperor and appointed Supreme Counsellor at the imperial palace. He had been absent for thirteen years, from 139 to 126 BC. Of the hundred men who set out with him, only one returned.

The diplomatic stalemate resulting from Zhang Qian's mission had some important consequences, as much political and military as commercial. Zhang Qian revealed to the emperor that, during his time in Bactra, he had noticed some bamboo canes and some fabrics that had come from what are now the Chinese provinces of Sichuan and Yunnan, which merchants were going to buy in Northern India. Zhang Qian therefore proposed to seek a direct southern route to Bactria which would avoid the regions inhabited by the Xiongnu. The emperor accordingly put forward the idea of making peace with those countries

The emperors of China were often shown in an identical posture, accompanied by two aides. This fixed portrayal is found even in wall paintings of the Dunhuang caves. Here, the emperor Wu of the Northern Zhou (reigned AD 561 – 578).

that appreciated the rich goods of the Han, and sought to establish diplomatic and economic relations with them. By means of gifts and privileges, he reasoned, it should be possible to make a favourable impression on these states and at the same time expand the influence of the Han empire and its excellence to other countries. These were therefore the motives for the orders he would give. Several

Between 139 and 126 BC, Zhang Qian made his way to the Yuezhi (Indo-Scythians). His journey is illustrated here by a painting in Dunhuang cave 323. It was carried out under the Tang, and has Buddhist subjects as its neighbours.

9

missions were entrusted with the task of seeking out approach routes, especially to the south. When they did so, however, they encountered a number of different tribes who killed and robbed the Han envoys.

A few years later, Zhang Qian set off once more on his journey and made his way to the Wusun, in the Ili valley. Although they had been the subjects of the Xiongnu, the Wusun had now drawn somewhat apart from them. If, thought Zhang Qian, they are offered gifts, and if a Chinese princess is sent for their king to marry, it might well be possible to turn them against the Xiongnu. And if ties were made with the Wusun, other states should do the same. A delegation of 300 men was therefore organised, with Zhang Qian at its head. Each man had two horses. They took cattle and sheep with them, and made arrangements to offer gold, silken fabrics and other gifts in great quantities. Their request for an alliance met with an evasive reply. The Wusun certainly wished to get hold of a Chinese princess for their king, but they did not feel capable of challenging the Xiongnu openly. Zhang Qian therefore returned to Changan with horses by the

My family has married me from the other side of Heaven,
They have sent me far to a foreign land, to the king of the Wusun.
My house is a tent, and felt forms its walls,
Meat is my food, and fermented milk its sauce.
I think constantly of my native land, my heart is quite bruised,
I would like to be a golden swan in order to return to my homeland.

POEM BY LIU XIJUN,
a princess given in marriage to the king of the Wusun, about 110–105 BC. In "Han Shu", 96B.

Chinese princesses were sent to the Xiongnu, and even to the Wusun, where they were married to their leaders. This took place regularly under the Han. By way of exchange, the sons of the 'barbarian' sovereigns were welcomed to the Chinese capital as a means of guaranteeing good relations.

dozen as a present for the emperor. The king of the Wusun would thus soon obtain a Chinese princess, who would become his Right-Hand Lady. For good measure, the Xiongnu would equally send him a girl to marry who would become his Left-Hand Lady. A thousand horses would be offered in exchange for the princess, who in return would bring a quantity of silken goods. To console her, the emperor would frequently send her brocades and silken garments.

At the time of his mission to the Wusun, Zhang Qian had sent envoys to other kingdoms, to Parthia and India. From then on, missions were despatched regularly, the most important of them having several hundred participants. Every year, from five to ten missions left China.

At the same time, the kingdoms sent their own emissaries. One delegation, from Arsacide Persia, came to Changan with ostrich eggs and conjurors from Ligan, a place that some took to be Alexandria in Egypt, others Petra in Syria, and others again Hyrcania, to the south-west of the Caspian Sea.

The diplomatic missions sometimes departed from their objective. It was not always easy to find participants who were men of good repute. Increasingly frequently, the delegates were infiltrated by people who were less scrupulous than they should have been, and who ignored the imperial orders and appropriated for themselves the gifts that they bore. They then sold these for their own gain.

The first such tentative exchanges, in among Zhang Qian's adventures, show what the original Chinese concept of foreign relations was, whether political or commercial. Neighbouring kingdoms, or rather city-states, had to be won over by gifts. And in becoming a sort of foreign vassal state, they increased the influence of the Han. That was why the missions took gold and generous supplies of silken goods with them. To maintain good relations princesses were sent as

The barbarian horse with russet ears
Shakes his head, tosses his ears, swings his golden reins.
Not long since, he fought many times, the battle field was broad;
With the long lance, the

horsemen returned to the frontier.
When he went into battle,
Sweat flowed from him like blood.
Everyone gave a single shout to call a halt.
At the end of the battle, when the pennons were rolled up,
His sweat dried up;
His golden saddle was taken off.

PELLIOT,
Chinese manuscripts 3911 and 2809

concubines for the rulers of the vassal states and, in exchange, members of the ruling families of the states were obliged to come and live as hostages in the Chinese capital. This policy of exchanging gifts could have become ruinous for the Han economy, since it represented almost a third of the imperial revenue in the 1st century AD. Instead, however, it served as a stimulus to commercial exchanges, thanks to the trade that developed — a trade based largely on silk.

Li Guangli and the Celestial Horses

The celestial horses arrive,
Coming from the far east.
They have crossed the moving
sands,
The nine barbarians have been
overthrown.
The celestial horses arrive,
Springing from the water of a
single spring.
Like tigers, their backbone is
double,
They are changing like demons.
The celestial horses arrive,
They have passed through places
without grass,
Crossing a thousand *li*
To come from distant regions.
The celestial horses arrive,
This very year precisely.
Are they preparing to spring
At who knows what moment?

in "Han Shu", 22

Zhang Qian had told the emperor about some horses that sweated blood which he had seen in the Ferghana Valley and which he believed to be the descendants of supernatural horses, celestial horses. The emperor had originally been well satisfied with the Wusun horses, which he had called 'Celestial Horses'. An oracle had revealed that the supernatural horses came from the north-west. When he learned that there were even better horses in the Ferghana Valley, he renamed the Wusun horses as 'Horses of the Far West', keeping the name 'Celestial Horses' for those that came from Ferghana.

Envoys had reported on their return that in the town of Ershi, capital of the Dayuan region (that is, the medieval town of Sutrishna, near Uratepe, between Khodzhent and Samarkand), there had been magnificent horses that could not be shown to them. Wudi appointed an envoy to go with a thousand gold coins and a golden horse. But the king of Dayuan, weary of the Chinese envoys, and feeling remote enough from China for troops to be unable to make him submit, refused to supply the precious horses. The envoy, in anger, smashed the golden horse that he had brought as a gift. Soon after he was murdered and stripped.

The incident caused a considerable stir, and Emperor Wu charged Li Guangli, promoted in advance to be general in command of Ershi, to bring the king of Dayuan to his senses and to take possession of the horses. Thus in 104 BC, at the head of 6000 horsemen and thousands of reasonably disciplined foot soldiers, Li Guangli set off to punish the kingdom of Dayuan. But the campaign failed. The army was short of provisions, and all along their route the Han warriors were unable to obtain the supplies that they sought in the towns through which they passed. Exhausted, the soldiers reached the borders of Dayuan, but were unable to capture the city of Yucheng where the Chinese envoy had been

Near Jiayuguan, in the Hexi Corridor, an obligatory passage of the Silk Road, several tombs decorated with 3rd-century wall paintings were discovered in 1972. Above, a procession on horseback.

killed. Li Guangli was thus forced to retreat to Dunhuang, after losing most of his troops. From there, he sent a messenger to the emperor to inform him of the situation and to ask him to disband the troops while awaiting reinforcements. The emperor ordered him to remain encamped outside the Jade Gate of Yumenguan and forbade the soldiers to return to China.

After some indecision, Wudi, keen to obtain the famous horses, and reckoning that this setback would give an impression of weakness to the other kingdoms, decided to send reinforcements. The expedition comprised 60,000 soldiers, not including servants carrying personal goods, 100,000 head of cattle, over 30,000 horses, and thousands of donkeys and camels. Two experts were assigned the task of selecting the horses once Dayuan had been conquered.

On arriving at the outskirts of Ershi, the royal capital, which he had planned to besiege, Li Guangli learned that the town had no well. He therefore diverted the course of the river which supplied the town with water. The siege lasted forty days. Inside the city, there was a state of riot. Some inhabitants claimed that the war had been caused by the king's order to kill the Han envoy. If they therefore killed the king in return, and offered the horses to the Han, the siege would be lifted. And that was what happened. Li Guangli accepted the terms. He ordered scores of the best horses to be selected as well as 3000 ordinary stallions and mares. A treaty was agreed: two celestial horses would be sent every year. The Han would also take back supplies of lucerne seed and vine plants. The two campaigns had lasted four years.

It has sometimes been suggested that Wudi's wish to obtain the celestial horses of Ferghana was associated with the quest for immortality which he pursued. The celestial horses were said to have emerged from a river, just as the famous dragon-horse came out of the Yellow River bearing the great mythical map (the *Luoshu*) on its back, with the map showing the extent of its authority. It is also possible that the need to obtain stallions arose from the wish to replenish the Han cavalry, which had been decimated as a result of the battles against the Xiongnu. It appears in general that the celestial horses never really became acclimatised in China, even when the lucerne seeds had been brought back and sown in various places.

In the tomb of a Later Han general discovered at Leitai, near Wuwei, in 1969, more than 200 funerary objects were discovered. One of them became instantly famous, the flying horse, with one hoof balancing on a swallow.

Diplomacy and Commerce

As a result of Li Guangli's expedition, the neighbouring kingdoms had taken fright and sent both tributes and hostages to the Chinese court. It was at about this period that the four commanderies of Jiuquan, Zhangye, Dunhuang and Wuwei were founded, in order to back up the Chinese penetration into Central Asia. The latter was chiefly the work of Pan Chao (AD 31–103), who waged constant war over the whole of present-day Turkistan in order to subdue the many kingdoms which were being constantly set up, either as allies of the Chinese or as allies of the Xiongnu. The political parcelling out of the Tarim basin and of Central Asia simply had the effect of increasing their size. At the beginning of the Han dynasty there were thirty-six kingdoms in all, but by the start of the Christian era there were at least fifty.

It was also at this time that commercial exchanges increased considerably. Little information is available on these trading activities, since literate Chinese harboured a deep disdain for trade in general. The goods brought by foreign emissaries were regarded as tributes which, when assembled in the imperial treasury, would testify to the size and extent of the empire. In the reign of Wudi,

In the distance are the
barbarians of the West,
In a region beyond Heaven.
The goods of their countries are
valuable and beautiful,
But the nature of the inhabitants
is lawless and weak.
They do not observe the rites of
China,
Not one possesses books to give
the rules.
If they did not have their
religion,
What would save them?
What would check them?

FAN YE,
"Hou Han Shu", 88

the palace would have housed luminous pearls, cowrie shells, rhinoceros horn and kingfisher feathers. Later, the imperial possessions would include all kinds of horses (*pushao* horses, dragonlike horses, 'fish-eyed' horses, blood-sweating horses) as well as elephants, lions, ostriches and the like.

The reality was sometimes more harsh. Merchants became members of Chinese missions and expeditions, and in AD 94, for example, when General Pan Chao launched a military expedition against the kingdom of Yanqi (Karashar), several hundred merchants joined his forces.

But above all, delegations from foreign kingdoms arriving at the imperial court were frequently composed exclusively of merchants making false claims on behalf of sovereigns of remote states. It was thus that in the reign of Chengdi (32 – 7 BC) allegations were made that among the delegations who had come to pay allegiance to the Han there was not a single member of a royal family, nor even a nobleman. The majority of the emissaries were merchants coming to barter their merchandise and carry out trading under the pretence of offering gifts. In the same way, in AD 166, a merchant passing himself off as an emissary from the Roman emperor Marcus Aurelius Antoninus arrived in Tonkin to offer elephant tusks, rhinoceros horn and tortoiseshell, although these were things which by then were no longer regarded as really valuable.

A wall painting in Dunhuang cave 103. It dates from the Tang period and illustrates the parable of the imaginary town. On the fragment shown here, a caravan is led by an elephant.

Routes

The commercial exchanges which thus developed with the West were influenced not only by changes in the political attitude but by the geographical situation. In order to reach Sogdiana, Bactria, Parthia or India, the merchants had to cross deserts and mountains. Oases were essential as points of passage.

Under the Han, two routes could be used for trading purposes. They both began in Yumenguan and Yangguan. The first, in the south, passed through Shanshan (Loulan) and made its way west, skirting the mountains to the Congling Mountains, the 'Onion Mountains', otherwise the Pamirs, and so to the Yuezhi and the Parthians. The history of the Later Han notes that after Shanshan, the route crossed the kingdoms of Qiemo (Cherchen), Jingjue (Niya), Jumi (or Wumi), Pishan, Yutian (Khotan), and Xiye (Yarkand). It adds that from Pishan, travelling south-west, one came to the kingdom of Jibin (Kashmir), then from there to Quyishanli, otherwise Alexandria (?Herat) and Tiaozhi (perhaps Taoke, near Bushire, on the Persian Gulf).

The second route, in the north, passed through Jushi (Turfan), and skirting the northern mountains, led to Shule (Kashgar). Continuing westwards, one passed the Congling Mountains (Pamirs) and reached Dayuan (Ferghana), Kangju (Samarkand) and Yancai (probably corresponding to the place where the *Aorsoi* lived, the people mentioned by Strabo who were the ancestors of the Alemanni). It is known that at the close of the Earlier Han dynasty, in AD 2, the northern route was divided in the region of Jushi (Turfan) in order to avoid the Dunes of the White Dragons (Bailong Dui), between Hami and Turfan. These white sand dunes had the appearance of headless dragons.

In reality, the routes themselves are not so easy to trace. In the 3rd century, Yu Huan, in his *Weilüe* (Summary of the History of the Wei), informs us that there were three routes. The southern route is still the same, while the northern route becomes the central route. Yu Huan tells how, on leaving Yumenguan from the west, with the Well of the Protector (Duhu Jing) as the starting point, the route ascends through the northern edge of the Desert of the Three Hills (Sanlong Sha) and leads past the Julu granary. Then at the Shaxi well, it veers

north-west, crossing the Dragon Dunes to arrive in ancient Loulan, and from there goes further west to reach Qiuzi (Kucha) and the Congling Mountains.

This bas-relief, preserved in the Palmyra Museum, shows laden dromedaries lying down. Dromedaries are the Arabian cousins of the so-called Persian or 'Bactrian' camel.

As far as the new northern route is concerned, the texts are not clear. Either it appears to follow the course of the central route between Yumenguan and Turfan, where the two routes divide, or else we are given to believe that it was quite a different route. Chavannes claimed that it made its way northwards in the direction of Hami, after which it crossed the mountains and emerged by Lake Barköl, from where it continued west skirting the northern edge of the Tien Shan.

These three routes were more likely to have been the principal axes of a number of crossing and dividing roads. The northern route by the Tien Shan, for example, must have linked up with the route south of the Tien Shan to join it in the region of Turfan. The routes operating under the Han are only known to us as they applied to the regions that roughly correspond to the present province of Xinjiang, that is, to those regions that were under the control of the Chinese. Beyond that, legend takes over and blends with the factual knowledge that the Chinese then had of the West. It is true that, as seen from the capital, journeys along these routes were fraught with dangers of all kinds. Apart from the instability that resulted from the constant collapse of the kingdoms in the 'western districts', natural difficulties also had to be taken into account. This was the situation as described by Du Qin under the Earlier Han with regard to relations with the kingdom of Jibin (Kashmir):

'On leaving Pishan for the south, one crosses four or five kingdoms which are not subject to the Han. A party of a hundred men can divide the night into five watches, banging on their eating bowls and keeping a lookout, for there may well be chances of being attacked and robbed. As for donkeys, cattle and provisions, one is dependent on the richness of the various kingdoms. Some kingdoms are too poor or too small to provide food, or are too cruel and deceitful to give anything. Thus our emissaries, who bear tablets from the powerful Han, die of hunger in the mountains and valleys. They beg without receiving anything so that, after ten to twenty days, men and beasts are abandoned in the desert without being able to return. Moreover, they pass through the Mountains of the Great Headache and the Little Headache and along the slopes of the Red Land and the Land of Fever. They are stricken with fever and lose their colour. They have a severe headache and vomit. It is the same for the donkeys and cattle. Again, there are the Three Ponds and the slopes of the Great Rocks where the footpath is only eighteen or nineteen inches wide (about 40 cm) for a distance of thirty *li*. It runs along the edge of a precipice of unfathomable depth. Whether on horseback or on foot, travellers hold on to one another and pull one another along with ropes. It is only after more than two thousand *li* that one comes to the Suspended Passages. When animals fall, before even reaching halfway across the ravine, they are dashed to pieces. When men fall, they are unable to save themselves. The danger of these precipices is greater than anything else' (*Hou Han Shu,* 96 A).

The dangers of travelling by land were not the only ones. A journey by sea could be even more fearful. That, at least, is what the Parthians gave Gan Ying cause to believe in AD 97. General Pan Yao had sent him on a mission to the land of Daqin, otherwise known as the Roman Empire. Gan Ying arrived at Tiaozhi and, finding himself on the edge of a great sea, wished to cross it, but sailors from Anxi (Parthia) told him: 'The sea is too big. A crossing can take three months if the winds are favourable, but if the winds are contrary, it can take two years. So those who set sail on this sea take provisions for three years. In mid-ocean, one suffers from homesickness, and many die of it.' Hearing this, Gan Ying abandoned his plans. It appears that the Parthians deliberately set out to scare Gan Ying, for it was important for them to prevent direct relations being established between China and the Roman Empire, since the silk trade passed via themselves as middlemen. Such at any rate was the impression of the Chinese: 'The king of Daqin constantly desired to send merchants to the Han, but the Parthians wished to trade Chinese silken goods with him; that was why they set up obstacles and hindered any kind of communication'.

Ostia controlled the basic imports and exports of Rome, and was the terminal point for all routes from the east, whether by land between the Levant and China, or by sea to India.

ROME AND THE SERES

The silk which reached Rome in the 1st century BC came from a mysterious country, the land of the Seres, of which nothing was originally known other than that it was inhabited by people who made silk, produced by a sort of 'wool tree'. In point of fact, the Seres were then as much people who made silk as people who sold it. The Seres were sometimes confused with the Scythians, the Indians or the Parthians. This was because silk was conveyed not only through the Parthians, by a land route, but also by Indian ships.

India and the Sea Routes

In the course of his journey to the Yuezhi, Zhang Qian had come across bamboo and fabrics. It is not known whether the latter included any silk materials. But one thing is certain that trade had existed for a long time between Southern China and Northern India via Burma, also perhaps by sea. The presence of silk in India was recorded as early as the 4th century BC by Panini. With the opening of the routes in Central Asia that followed the missions of Zhang Qian, trade with India began to flourish. Proof of this can be found in archaeological discoveries, such as the piece of silk with an inscription in Brahmi writing discovered by Aurel Stein in a watchtower at Yumenguan. Subsequently, it would be learned that the kingdom of Khotan appeared to have played a major role as an intermediary in commercial activities.

India, too, played a similar role in the trade between Rome and China, as also did Parthia, which to some extent was in competition with the former country. Trading via sea routes tended to supersede trade by land routes, especially from the 2nd century AD. This was a consequence of the wars between Rome and the Parthians, from the time of the Battle of Carrhae (53 BC) to the advance of Trajan between AD 114 and 117. The severity of the taxes levied by the Parthians as payment for their commercial mediation was not without influence in the decision to launch the latter campaign. Trade was organised in several stages, first from China to India, then from India to Egypt or Syria and to Rome. Silk reached India either through Central Asia, or via Burma, or perhaps following the Indo-Chinese coasts and passing through the Malacca Straits.

From the western coasts of India, several routes were active. It was doubtless initially Arab ships that made their way through the Red Sea and across the Indian Ocean. The Arabs were renowned for their commercial activities and also famous for their acts of piracy. As Pliny the Elder (AD 23 – 79) states in his *Natural History:* 'One half lives in trading and the other half in brigandry; in short, they are the richest nation in the world, for the treasures of the Romans and the Parthians flow there. The Arabs sell the products of their seas and their forests and buy nothing.'

It was later from Egypt that ships were laden for India, competing with the Arab boats. Strabo (58 BC – AD 21) tells how in the early years of the Christian era 120 ships set sail every year from Myos Hormos for India. Pliny describes a route from another point of departure, Alexandria. Leaving from Alexandria, ships made their way to Juliopolis, from where they sailed up the Nile to Coptos (Kuft), a journey that took twelve days. The journey then continued by caravan to the port of Berenice (Bender el Kebir) on the Red Sea, where the travellers embarked. The journey was mostly made at night because of the heat. The route next led to Ocelis (probably Seh Sa'id, in the Bab el Mandeb Strait) in southern Arabia, and on to Muziris in India (Kodungalur), taking forty days. About three months were thus needed to travel from Alexandria to India. The ships' crews took advantage of the so-called Hippal wind, or monsoon. A certain Hippal, in about 100 BC, had discovered the advantage to be gained from these seasonal winds which, no doubt, the Indians and the Arabs knew of before him.

Cargoes that have come from the Indians and even those from the fortunate Arabians can be seen here in such great quantity that one can easily imagine that nothing is left with those peoples, save trees stripped of their leaves, and that if they wish to obtain their own products, they must come and beg for them here. The fabrics of Babylon and the jewels of the far barbarian countries arrive here in great number and more easily than the products of Naxos or Cythnos arrive at Athens.

AELIUS ARISTIDES,
"Eulogy on Rome"

What good to you are these Stoic treaties which linger on Seric cushions?

HORACE,
"Epodes", VIII, 15 – 16

As well as the route used by merchants from Alexandria, merchandise was also conveyed by other routes, such as the one which led from Leuke Kome on the Red Sea to Petra and Rhinocolura (Al Arish) on the Mediterranean, or the route which went to Petra via the Persian Gulf. Nor should the route which ran from the Oxus (Amu Darya) be overlooked. This often followed navigable courses through the Caspian Sea and Euxine (Black) Sea to Mesopotamia and Palmyra, or else led there overland.

It is clear that, despite its importance, silk was not the sole object of trade. From India also came ships bearing furs of Chinese origin, and iron. But in general boats setting sail from India were laden with spices and perfumes. Cinnamon from China or Ceylon, used for medicines or perfumes, was highly prized by the Romans, as was pepper. Pearls from the Red Sea, emeralds and incense also followed the sea routes. No ship would set off empty for the West. The Romans, for their part, exported basically glass to China. The Chinese believed that the wonderful objects which came from foreign kingdoms were almost all ultimately from Da Qin, otherwise the Roman Empire. As far as glass was concerned, there were ten different kinds of opaque glass depending on its colour: pink, white, black, green, yellow, blue, brown, azure, red or violet. Commercial exchanges, even so, were quite unequal, involving a massive outflow of valuable gold, even if not as radically as one might think. According to Pliny, one hundred million sesterces were thus transferred every year in trade with India, the Seres and Arabia. And a good proportion of this currency must have been involved in the purchase of silk.

Silk at Rome

The taste for silk, which had gradually been acquired from China, had been established in Rome in the 1st century BC. It was a luxury above all others. Silk was not initially used to make clothing. Originally, it was imported already in fabric form. Its great price caused it to be used for ornaments sewn on to clothing. Then it was used to decorate cushions. It was somewhat later that silk was used to make clothes. It seems that when this happened, silk was rewoven, mainly to make the light, transparent materials in which women so delighted, although men, too, sought silken clothing. Pliny tells us about this in his *Natural History* (VI, 54): 'The first men who were involved in it were the Seres, famous for the wool of their forests. They detach the white down from the leaves by sprinkling it with water, and so our women perform the double task of separating the strands and reweaving them. It is through such difficult work that one obtains from such a distant land that which enables a lady to appear in public in transparent dress'. It was against these indecent garments that first Seneca (AD 4 – 65), then Solinus (3rd century) took a stand.

Since the dawn of Christianity, the wearing of silk by men had been opposed as a decadent luxury. Under the consulate of Taurus and Libon, in AD 16, the Roman senate, Tacitus tells us, forbade men to 'disgrace themselves by the wearing of silk materials' (*Annals,* II, 33). Tiberius himself (reigned AD 14 – 37), in a letter to the senate, wished for a ban on these clothes 'which confuse men with

Women, take from me these garments covered in gold and purple; far from me the Tyrian purple, and the threads that the distant Seres gather from their trees.

SENECA,
"Phaedra", 387 – 389

It was the passion for luxury that led first women and now even men to use these fabrics which serve to reveal the body rather than to clothe it.

SOLINUS,
"Polyhistor", LI

women' (*Annals,* III, 53). But in vain. The fashion for fine fabrics had begun with the 'bombycine' which 'seric' first rivalled then superseded. Bombycine, a material woven with the thread of the wild silkworm from the island of Kos, has moreover been sometimes confused with silk from China, to the extent that Pliny uses the same formulae for his descriptions of the work of weaving (or reweaving). Aristotle had already described 'these horned caterpillars which weave in the manner of spiders the fabrics from which is made for the dress and adornment of women a material named bombycine'. Whatever confusion there may have been, Chinese silk had conquered Rome to clothe the aristocracy and to become as sought after as gold or porphyry. Despite its widespread use, its precise origin would long remain mysterious.

Geography

The knowledge that the Romans had of China was more than vague. If silk came to Rome, it was neither Chinese merchants who brought it, nor Roman traders who fetched it. This was doubtless why the exact location of the land of the Seres was little known, and was believed to be somewhere between the Scythians and the Indians. One of the only things that is known is the Roman custom of commercial exchange, which was carried out without a single word being spoken and even without any contact between buyer and seller. This is what Pomponius Mela (1st century BC) relates in his *Chorography:* 'Then come vast regions infested with wild beasts as far as Mount Tabis, which dominates the sea. At a great distance the Taurus rises. The distance which separates these two mountains is inhabited by the Seres, a nation full of justice and well known for the manner in which they carry on their trade, which consists in leaving the merchandise in a solitary place from where the purchaser conveys it when they are no longer present'.

The physical description of the Seres emphasises the confusion that prevailed in the Roman mind. One Rachias, an ambassador from Ceylon, explained, according to Pliny (*Natural History,* VI, 88), that the Seres 'exceeded the normal height, had red hair, blue eyes, a fearful voice, and did not speak to foreigners'. To this confusion of the Seres with, as it would seem, Indo-Europeans was added a confusion between two names: the Seres and the people of Kerala, on the west coast of India, where they were known in Tamil as *Cerar.*

These mysterious men were supposed to have a great longevity, over two hundred years according to Strabo (*Geography,* XV, 1, 20) and even three hundred years according to Lucian (2nd century BC): 'It is reported that the Seres live until the age of three hundred years. Some attribute this longevity to the air, others to the soil, others again to the diet. In fact it is said that the whole race drinks nothing but water'. It is worth noting that the astonishment of the westerners at the water-drinking Chinese was rivalled only by the astonishment of the Chinese at the wine-drinking western merchants.

This somewhat idyllic attitude reached its height with Bardesanes at the beginning of the 3rd century, when the land of the Seres is seen as a country of perfect moral laws: 'With the Seres, the law prohibits murder, prostitution, theft

The origin of the word China in ancient European languages derives from the name of the Qin dynasty, founded by the First Emperor, Shi Huangdi, in 221 BC. Its grandeur and fame were well known, even in the West.

and the worship of statues. In this huge land, one sees no temple, no prostitute, no adulterous woman, no thief under sentence, no murderer, no victim of a murder' (after Eusebius, *Preparation of the Gospel*).

The poor understanding of China that prevailed in the West in the first centuries of the Christian era is shown in the distinction that was made between the two Chinas that made silk, according, no doubt, to whether the silk came to Rome by land or sea. The *Periplus of the Erythrean Sea* tells of a country named 'Thin': 'There is in this country a very great inner city named Thinae, whence raw silk, thread and the material called *serikon* are brought on foot across Bactria to Barygaza, and by the Ganges to Limuria (in Asia Minor). It is not easy

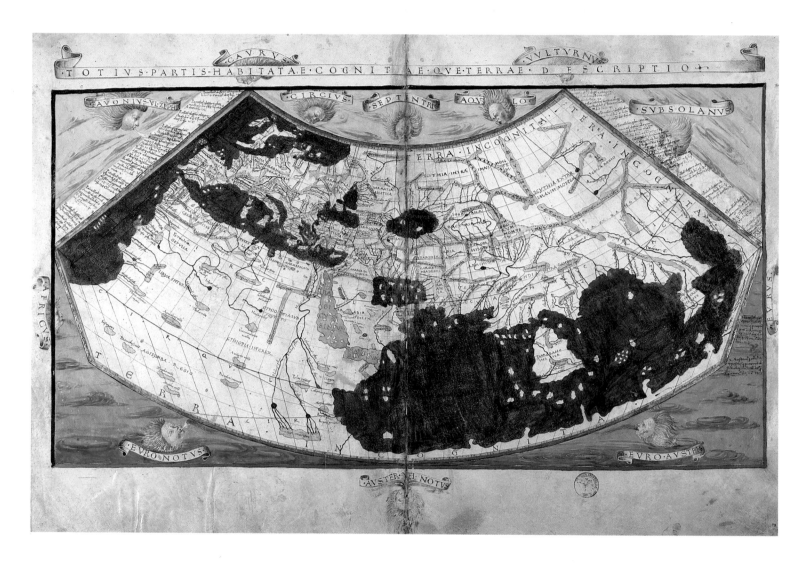

Map based on the description given by Ptolemy in his Geography *(c. AD 150) and drawn up in about 1400. It shows two Chinas: China in the proper sense of the name and Serica. The contours of the Far East are blurred into a vague area.*

to penetrate into this country, for there are only a few people who have returned from it, and that very rarely'.

Ptolemy (2nd century AD), setting out to correct Marinus of Tyre in his *Geography*, distinguishes the *Sinai* from the land of the Seres. Sera, the capital of the Seres, is seven months' march from the Stone Tower, a stage on the silk route. The land of the Seres, or Serica, 'is situated above the Sinai, to the west of whom is an unknown land, covered with slimy ponds, where great reeds grow so thick that the inhabitants use them to cross these swamps' (I, 17). The Sinai (the equivalent of the Thinae in the *Periplus*) were said to be to the south of Serica.

This distinction between the two Chinas remained long entrenched in the communal mind, since the voyage undertaken by Beneditto Goës at the beginning of the 17th century even then aimed to determine whether Cathay and China were one and the same country or not.

It must be said that the word *Thinae* (or *Sinai*), as applied to China, without any doubt derived, as did the Sanskrit *Cina,* from the Chinese term *Qin.* In fact, after the unification of China by the sovereign of the kingdom of Qin and the founding of the first centralised empire in 221 BC, the Chinese were known elsewhere in the world as the 'people of Qin'. A likely derivation for the name would appear later under the Liao dynasty (AD 907 – 1125), with this established by the Qidan or Kitai nomads in the north of China, and giving the name of Cathay. This latter name was the one by which western travellers of the 13th century such as Joannes de Plano Carpini and William de Ruysbroeck understood the whole of the Chinese world, and the name *Kitai* still remains today as the Russian word for China.

With regard to the name *Qin,* it is curious to note that the Chinese themselves designated the Romans by the name of 'Great Qin', *Da Qin,* and often attributed to them the same qualities that the Romans attributed to themselves: 'The people of this land are all inhabitants of great height, with regular features; they are similar to the inhabitants of the Middle Kingdom and that is why this country is called Da Qin' (*Hou Shan Shu,* 88). Their longevity was seen as important, as the Romans believed it to be for the Chinese. The Chinese even believed that the Romans grew mulberry trees and raised silkworms.

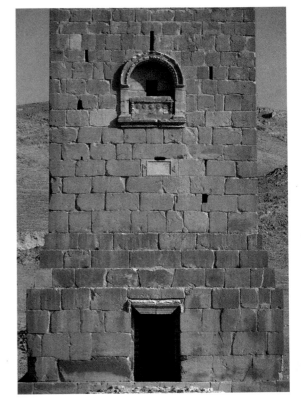

The knowledge that the Romans had of the land silk route was as vague as that of the Chinese. The first details of this route are known to us from the writings of Ptolemy, when he rebukes the geographer Marinus of Tyre, who had himself based his knowledge on that gained from a Macedonian merchant named Maes Titianos. This last had not gone in person to the Seres, but he had sent some of his men there and had himself made part of the route.

Several silken fabrics of Chinese origin have been discovered in the region of Palmyra. At Al-Bara, between Palmyra and Antioch, a tomb has also yielded silken cloths brought from China under the Han.

From Hierapolis (to the north of Aleppo), the route crossed Mesopotamia, passed over the Tigris and from there came to Ecbatana (Hamadan) and the Caspian Gates (a pass in the Elburz Mountains, east of Damavand). It then ran across Parthia to Hecatompylos (not very far from the present Damgan), and made its way towards Antioch of Margiana (no doubt Merv) and Bactra (Balkh). After Bactra, the route crossed the Komedoi Mountains (Pamirs) and reached the Stone Tower. This Stone Tower (*Lithinos pyrgos*) has been the cause of much spilt ink, and it is still unknown where exactly this staging and exchange point was. It may have been near the present Tashkurgan.

Ptolemy does not mention the route of the Silk Road from the Stone Tower to the 'Sera metropolis', but only gives the names of several towns. Some of them have been located: Scythian Issedon (Kucha), Damna (Kushar) on the route to the north of the Tarim, Seric Issedon (Loulan) on the southern route, then Daxata (Yumenguan) and Throana (Dunhuang) where the routes joined up.

The Stone Tower and the region of the Pamirs can be said to have formed the limit of the respective Roman and Chinese knowledge about the Silk Road. It is for this reason, perhaps, that the Stone Tower has often been taken to be the chief trading post between the caravans of China and those from the West.

The considerable impression that silk produced on the Romans no doubt stemmed as much from the qualities of the cloth as from the mystery that surrounded its origin and manufacture. Because of its lightness, its delicacy, its elegance, its suppleness and the richness of its woven patterns, silk had won over the aristocracy. Through its luxury, it had rightly come to replace the more usual clothing of wool or linen. This attraction for silk, with its distant origin, had the result of increasing its cost, already made high by the dangers of transportation and by the taxes and charges levied by the middlemen.

But what actually lay behind the object of this interest to the western world? We must now throw some light on the mystery.

THE WONDERFUL THREAD

THE HISTORY AND TECHNOLOGY OF SILK

Silk had been known in China from the earliest times. Its origin, as always, has been lost in the mists of time and in a number of intertangled myths. According to legend, it was the mythical emperor Fuxi who was the first to consider using silkworms and the mulberry to make clothes. It is Fuxi, too, who is credited with inventing a musical instrument whose strings were made of silk. Again, it is said that another legendary emperor, Shennong, 'the Farmer', had taught his people to grow the mulberry and hemp to make silk and cloth. Finally, it is claimed that it was Xiling, wife of Huangdi, the 'Yellow Emperor', who in the 3rd millennium BC taught people how to treat silk and cocoons in order to make clothes.

If the first attempts at sericulture and weaving remain unknown today, archaeological discoveries confirm their existence under the dynasty of the Shang (18th – 12th centuries BC). In 1958, at Qianshanyang, in the province of Zhejiang, fragments of silk were discovered in a bamboo basket. Carbon dating established that the fragments belonged to the 3rd millennium, that is, about 2750 BC. These appear to be the oldest silken fabrics yet known. They were the product of the domestic silkworm, *Bombyx mori.* In point of fact this dating has been to some extent challenged, especially by the Chinese archaeologist Xia Nai. In 1926, at Xiyicun in the province of Shanxi, a partly divided cocoon was discovered. It was dated back to the Yangshao culture, that is, to 2200 – 1700 BC. But this was not from the domestic silkworm, but from the wild silkworm, *Rondotia menciana* Moore. However, despite the evidence, some doubt has been cast on the authenticity of this discovery.

However it may be, mulberries, silkworms and silk have been attested from the pictograms found on bronzes and oracular bones of the Shang dynasty. In addition, according to the *Shangshu,* the 'Book of Writings', a collection of documents relating mainly to the history of the Zhou dynasty (12th – 3rd centuries BC), silk featured in the production and taxation imposed in several regions of China, corresponding to the present provinces of Shandong, Henan, Hebei, Shanxi, Anhui, Shaanxi and Jiangsu.

One can only guess at the production methods used for silk under the Shang and Zhou dynasties, as the main evidence is in fragments or traces of silk found adhering to bronze utensils, which were wrapped in silk and placed in tombs. In a few instances, later discoveries revealed similar evidence. The methods used for silk manufacture are only really known to us from Chinese texts of the 13th and 14th centuries AD, and it must be admitted that the growing of the mulberry and the breeding of silkworms have not significantly changed since ancient times.

Silk is obtained from the thread unwound from the cocoons made by silkworm larvae fed on mulberry leaves. But sericulture requires special conditions in order to produce good quality silk, and that no doubt is the source of the mystery and secrecy in which the process is shrouded.

First, the mulberry. Among the different kinds of mulberry tree that grow in China, it is the white mulberry, *Morus alba,* with its thick, broad leaves, which is selected to provide food for the silkworm. Moreover, there are two types of white mulberry, one wild, one cultivated. As the wild mulberry gives silk of only inferior quality, the traditional practice has evolved of growing sturdy wild mulberry trees, but of then grafting cultivated mulberries on to them. After only five years from planting, the leaves can be picked to be given to the silkworm to eat. Manuals on mulberry-growing now give a whole range of extremely precise instructions regarding methods of planting, cutting, layering, grafting, and so on.

Similarly, among the many different types of silkworm, it is specifically *Bombyx mori* which has been cultivated to provide the best silk.

In the fourth month, that is, at the moment when the leaves of the mulberry begin to sprout, the eggs of the silkworm, until then kept in a cool place, are put out to hatch in a warmer spot, or sometimes under blankets or clothing. Hatching takes place rapidly. It is very important that all the silkworms hatch at the same time, and for this reason there are procedures for hastening or retarding the hatching process. After hatching, the silkworms are laid out, as far as possible separately from one another, on screens covered with chopped straw. There, for food, they are given finely cut mulberry leaves at regular intervals,

The mythical emperor Fuxi, and Nugua, traditionally said to have been his sister or daughter, were believed to have created human beings. They are often shown entwined. Nugua is credited with the invention of marriage, while Fuxi is said to have been the 'inventor' of silk clothing.

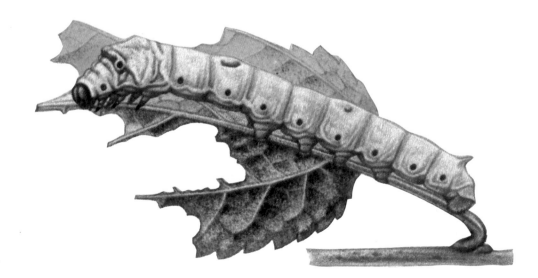

Bombyx mori is the only butterfly or moth to have been domesticated for the production of silk. Even if several other species of lepidoptera can be used, Bombyx mori is the only one to have been bred systematically for this purpose since earliest times.

day and night, for 35 days. During this period they moult four times, consuming ever increasing amounts of mulberry leaves after each moulting. Their length over the same period has increased from about two millimetres to five centimetres, and they are capable of consuming almost twenty times their own weight of leaves over the course of their life. Almost thirty mulberry trees are thus needed to obtain three kilos of unwound silk.

The silkworms then begin to spin their cocoons, after being transferred to other screens, which are equipped with straw cones and are frequently heated to avoid damp. The spinning takes a few days. The cocoons to be used for breeding are removed, and ten days later the silkmoths pierce the casing and emerge. Male and female moth then mate. The male dies soon after, while the female lays her eggs. These are collected and stored in a cool place for the production cycle to begin all over again. The remaining cocoons, meanwhile, provide the silk thread after unwinding. The best quality silk comes from cocoons that are firm and

Of the many kinds of mulberry tree, the white mulberry, Morus alba, *is the one that is best adapted for the production of silk. As it bears neither flower nor fruit, the essence of the tree is concentrated in the growth of its leaves. So says the Chinese encyclopaedia* Tiangong Kaiwu, *written in the 17th century.*

Bombyx mori is a heavy moth, incapable of flight. It does not take any food, and its sole function, in the course of its short life, is reproduction. Each female lays about 500 eggs.

white. They are either exposed to hot steam or are plunged into a bowl of hot water. This is the purification process. It has the effect of aiding the unwinding or reeling operation by softening the cocoon and partly ridding it of sericin, which is the gelatinous substance that binds the silk strands together. The pupating larva is killed before the unwinding stage, either by keeping the cocoons under layers of salt or simply by heating them.

Only those cocoons that are whole and unbroken are used for reeling, and pierced or stained cocoons are simply cut and spun to make scrap silk. The actual unwinding is carried out with the aid of a comb that grips the filaments. The first filaments are used for the floss-silk that lines clothing and quilts. The continuous thread from the cocoon, sometimes more than 1500 metres long, is wound onto the reeling machine without any tension being applied. The filaments of different cocoons are gathered on the winder one after the other. For a kilo of silk, more than ten kilos of cocoons are needed.

The silk manufacturing process demands very great care, as laid down in the manuals on silkworm breeding. The silkworms themselves are sensitive to noise, smell, wind, changes in temperature, the cleanliness of the people who handle them, and the like. One of these factors, temperature, was something of which the Romans were certainly aware, despite their great ignorance in the art of silk manufacture, and Strabo attributed the fact that the 'wool' grew on certain trees to the warmth of the climate.

The techniques of weaving, like the production of the silken thread, depend on a sophisticated procedure. Silk was found to be greatly superior to other

According to the Tiangong Kaiwu, *silkworm cocoons were of two colours, yellow and white, depending on the place of production. They also had various shapes, some like pumpkins, some like the fruit of the yew-tree, and others like nuts. The cocoons were named according to their appearance: pure white, striped, all black, spotted, etc. However, they all produced silk identically.*

The outside of the cocoon consists of a network of loose silk, while the inside is made of a single filament whose length can reach 1500 metres. The silk itself is the product of two serigenic glands, and is essentially an excretion produced by the digestive waste of the silkworm.

natural fibres, which was doubtless one of the reasons for its attraction for western weavers, and which certainly influenced their methods of weaving. As noted by the art historian William Willetts, silk provides a yarn that is particularly strong. The density of the individual yarns per centimetre is twice or three times greater than any other fibre. The silk warp is now 'subjected to repeated impacts of the comb which teases the weft at the point where the fabric is formed'. The absence in the west of a firm warp was an obstacle to the perfecting of the fabric and explains the predominance of weft over warp in most ancient western fabrics. Silk was thus often used as a mixed weave in the Middle East and the

West, with the silken threads combined with those of linen or wool to serve as the weft. Examples of such mixed weave have been discovered at Palmyra.

The oldest method of weaving seems to have been by the use of stretchers. Pieces of a bronze loom used for such weaving and probably dating from the 2nd century BC have been found at Shizhishan in the province of Yunnan. From the time of the Shang dynasty to that of the Han, several types of loom superseded one another. The horizontal foot loom, which appeared under the Han, improved the technical aspect of the process and enriched the silk fabric with new types of weave. The cross weave gave way to damask, found widely under the Han, in which the pattern is visible only at the point of weaving. This effect was in general obtained by passing the warp thread over three weft yarns, then over one weft yarn, then again over three yarns, and so on. Shot silk, which requires a much more complex weaving process, probably made its first ap-

The operation of producing silk and breeding silkworms was rigorously and meticulously prepared. It became the subject of an important literature and iconography, as is shown, for example, by the famous plates of the Gengzhi Tu, *the 'Pictures of tilling and weaving', in which sericulture is raised to the same status as agriculture. Various stages of sericulture can be seen here: the gathering of mulberry leaves, the selecting of the cocoons that will be used to spin the silk, the monitoring of the cocoons, the unwinding of the cocoons, then the preparation of the thread and the dyeing of the silk.*

pearance during the period of the Warring States (403 – 222 BC), but did not spread significantly under the Han. Patterns were mostly worked in the direction of the weave. Several silk fabrics dating from this period have been recovered and analysed. For the most part they are fabrics originating as gifts or tributes, like those discovered in Mongolia and Siberia, at Noin-Oula, Ilmova-Pad, Pazyryk and Oglakty, or like the fabrics discovered on the Silk Road and probably originating from commercial transactions, such as those from Juyan

(Edsengol), Dunhuang, Loulan and Niya in China, Begram in Afghanistan, Kerch in the Crimea, and Dura-Europos or Palmyra in Syria.

Silk was dyed either in sections of fabric for single-colour silks, or as thread for shot silk fabrics. The method used in batik, which consists in tying the fabric at certain points in order to preserve it from the dye colour, appeared only some time after the Han period.

Under the Tang dynasty (AD 618 – 907) a new technique of weaving appeared in China, under the influence of the Sassanids of Persia. Patterns that were clearly of Persian inspiration were adopted and spread as far as Japan. Such patterns were no longer woven into the warp but into the woof, as was usual with weavers in the Middle East. The patterns consisted of palm-leaves and Arabian-style ornamentations, as well as grapes, the tree of life, or animals at bay, and especially scenes from lion hunts.

Silkworms dislike eating wet leaves. They dislike eating hot leaves. When they have just been born, silkworms dislike having fish or meat fried nearby. They dislike (rice) being pounded. They dislike resonant objects being struck. It is not to their liking when a women who has given birth less than a month previously is their foster-mother. They dislike it when a man carrying wine gives them mulberry leaves to eat, or takes them and lays them on the cloths. From birth to maturity, silkworms dislike smoke and smells. They dislike the smell of wine and of the five bitter plants. They dislike rancid smells, the smell of fish or musk, etc. They dislike it when, in the daytime, a window is opened in the direction of the wind. They

dislike the light of the setting sun. When it is hot, they dislike a violent wind or a sharp cold. When it is cold, they dislike a sudden and excessive heat. They dislike it when dirty people come into the breeding-house.

WANG ZEHN, *14th century, in "Shoushi Tongkao", 73*

Under the Shang dynasty, silk manufacture seems to have been concentrated in the hands of the imperial household, and again, under the Zhou, it was limited to the aristocracy. Silk served primarily in the ornamentation of clothing used for official ceremonies. Silken fabrics were offered as gifts by the king or queen to noble personages who had rendered a particular service. It then gradually became a form of currency, and later still a means of payment. Under the Zhou, for example, five slaves were exchanged for a horse and a skein of silk yarn.

Xuanzang had told how the people of Khotan wove silken cloths and fabrics as early as the 7th century. Even today, the silk industry is an important activity in the city, and 1500 employees work in the silk production shops.

Even if the unwinding of cocoons is now to some extent mechanised, the process has basically remained the same. According to the Tiangong Kaiwu, a reeling machine was used. A vessel of boiling water was used to kill the pupa, soften the cocoon, and dissolve the sericin. The roughness or fineness of the reeled thread depended on the number of cocoons thrown into the water at the same time. One person could unwind up to thirty ounces of silk thread a day (more than 1 kilo), but if the silk was destined to make turbans, only twenty ounces (about 750 grams) were unwound, otherwise the filaments would have been too long. For damask and gauze, only twenty cocoons were thrown into the water at once, and for turbans, only about ten went in. The water was stirred so that the end of the thread remained visible and also so that, if the thread broke, the remaining length could be pulled out. This method was the one used at Huzhou, in Zhejiang. In the province of Sichuan, the reeling machine was located directly over the hot water, and four or five threads could be unwound simultaneously. It is likely to have been this latter method that formed the basis of the one used today in Khotan.

The theme of the hunter on horseback drawing his bow is one of Sassanid origin that was common all along the Silk Road, from Japan in the east to France in the west, as on this fabric in the abbey at Mocaz.

The very great importance of silk and the reverence that the Chinese had had for this fine product since the earliest times are revealed in its etymology. A term such as *jing,* which was used to designate the classic writings of Confucianism and later the Buddhist *sutra,* originally represented a kind of comb used to prepare silk yarn. The character *zhi,* 'to govern', was initially used to denote the reeling. The word *luan,* 'chaos', 'disorder', represented tangled threads, and so on.

The sacrificial rites practised in honour of the divinity of the Silkworm, which we know about from oracular bones dating from the 13th and 12th centuries BC, testify to the place of silk in the social and economic life of China under the Shang. Popular worship was later attached to a goddess protector of

Fragment of a painting discovered near Khotan. It was immediately identified by Aurel Stein as illustrating the legend of the passing down of silk from China to the kingdom of Khotan. A princess given in marriage to the king of Khotan has mulberry seeds and silkworms concealed in her headdress.

silkworms and mulberries, the Girl Silkworm, Cannü, better known under the name of the 'Lady of the Horse's Head', Matou Shang. The legend behind this is somewhat unusual. In the time of the mythical emperor Gaoxin, the father of Cannü was captured by robbers, when his horse returned alone to its stable. Cannü's mother vowed that she would give her daughter's hand to whoever brought back her father. As no one was prepared to undertake this, the horse sprang off to seek for Cannü's father and brought him back. Once returned, the horse began to neigh incessantly and refused to eat or drink. The father angrily killed the horse, then dried its hide in the courtyard. But when his daughter passed by there, the horse's hide leapt up, wrapped itself round her, and flew off with her to perch on a mulberry tree, where Cannü was changed into a silkworm. It was chiefly in the province of Sichuan that the Lady of the Horse's Head was worshipped.

Passing on the Secret

The transferral of sericulture techniques to the West was particularly slow, as it also was for several other types of manufacture, especially that of paper. The infrequent chronological milestones are once again mostly of legendary origin. The description of western lands in the Dynastic Histories of China gives a bare mention of the manufacture of silk in the regions of Turkistan before the 5th century. True, it is believed that silk was made from the silkworm in the Roman Empire, but it is likely that the description of customs by the 'Great Qin' was largely fabricated. Among all the kingdoms of Central Asia known to the Chinese, only those of Yanqi (Karashar) and Yutian (Khotan) are mentioned as having a bearing on the growing of mulberry trees or the breeding of silkworms and even then only from the 6th century onwards, as narrated in the *Weishu* (History of the Wei). In Yanqi, silkworms were bred, but not with the aim of making silk. The cocoons were merely used for padding or filling. As for Khotan, it is said that the royal lands were used for five different crops, as well as for mulberries and hemp. Did they also breed silkworms? Probably. At any rate, the famous Buddhist pilgrim Xuanzang (AD 602 – 664) tells the legend that was then current about the introduction of sericulture to Khotan:

The mulberry tree that is chosen in China to feed silkworms is the Morus alba. *Traditionally, sturdy wild mulberry trees were planted first, then cultivated mulberries were grafted on to them, producing thick, broad leaves.*

'At one time, the people of this land did not know of the mulberry and the silkworm. They enquired about them from the kingdom of the East that had them, and commanded an emissary to fetch them. At that time, the prince of the Eastern kingdom held fast to the secret and did not wish to reveal it. He had given strict instructions to the border guards not to let mulberry seeds or silkworms to be taken out. The king of Jusadanna (Khotan), in terms of humble address and observing respectful ritual, asked to take a wife in the eastern kingdom. The prince, who was of favourable disposition towards distant peoples, agreed to his request. The king of Jusadanna ordered an envoy to find a wife for him, advising him as follows: "Tell the royal princess of the East that our country has never possessed silk or quilting, and has had neither mulberry nor silkworm. These will be needed if she is to have clothes made." On hearing these words, the young girl secretly asked for mulberry seeds and silkworms and hid them in the lining of her headdress. When she arrived at the border, the head guard examined everywhere, but did not dare examine the princess's headdress. Thus she came to the kingdom of Jusadanna ... When spring came, the mulberry seeds were planted, and when the month of the silkworm drew near, care was taken to gather some food for them. At first, they were fed with various leaves, but soon the mulberries were covered with leaves. The queen then had a decree carved in stone: It is forbidden to kill the silkworms, and the cocoons must not be unwound until the silkmoths have flown.'

This story was repeated later in the *Tangshu,* the 'History of the Tang', without any indication regarding the period to which it related. It was probably about the middle of the 5th century. And which eastern kingdom was this? Was it China, as might be supposed, or was it a neighbouring country, as was written in the History of the Tang? It was probably China. At least, if another version of the same story is to be believed, this time in Tibetan, and occurring in the 'Prophecy of the Land of Li' (Khotan). A king of Khotan, named Vijaya Jaya, had taken to wife the daughter of a king of China, called Punyesvara. She had started to breed silkworms, having brought some eggs with her. But when the worms were not yet fully grown, the ignorant ministers took them to be poisonous snakes and became concerned about the dangers that the creatures could cause when they became bigger. The king therefore gave the order to set fire to the breeding-house. The queen, unable to explain to the king what the creatures really were, rescued a few silkworms and bred them in secret. She was thus able to obtain the silk and weave it, and brought the result to the king together with a full account of the matter. The king then repented of having killed the silkworms and founded a Buddhist monastery. It was thus that sericulture came to Khotan.

From Khotan, the art of silk manufacture would spread to the West. The knowledge that already existed in the West had gradually spread: in the 2nd century AD Pausanias gave a more exact description of silkmaking than hitherto, and no longer wrote about the 'wool' tree of his predecessors, even if his account was still remote from reality:

'As for the thread, from which the Seres make their clothing, it does not come from bark but from a different source, as follows. There exists in their country a little animal, called by the Greeks *ser,* but given another name by the Seres themselves. The size of this (animalcule) is double that of the great scarab. For the rest, it resembles the spiders which make their webs in the trees, and has eight legs like the spiders. The Seres breed these animals by building them cages suitable for the temperature of both winter and summer, and the work of these animals is a fine web which is found wrapped round their legs. Up to the age of four years, (the Seres) raise them by offering them millet as food. But in the fifth year − for they know that the creatures do not live longer − they give them a green reed to eat, until they burst, and it is in the inside of the corpse that the greater part of the thread is found' (*Description of Greece,* VI, 26).

It was only in the 6th century, however, that the art of sericulture became known in the West and came to be practised in the eastern Roman Empire at Constantinople. Its introduction here was basically prompted for economic reasons. The cost of silk had not lessened over the course of time, especially as demand for it was keen in Constantinople, where it was used not only for clothes but also for ornaments, liturgical robes, hangings, etc. Trade in silk was mainly in the hands of Persian merchants, who transported merchandise by land as well as by sea. Cargoes from India were regularly bought up by the Persians. This was why the emperor Justinian (reigned AD 527 − 565) had sought an opening to the Red Sea when making an alliance with the king of Axoum (Ethiopia). The wars with the Persians were not unrelated to the problems experienced by the Byzantine Empire in obtaining silk. The increase in silk prices resulted in the

At the time of the Renaissance, silk weaving became a major art. In France, the industry was first developed by Louis XI, but it was at Lyon under Francis I (1515 – 1547) that silk began to be developed as we now know it. Above, portrait of Francis I by Jean Clouet.

A robe of Chinese silk, dating probably from the Tang dynasty, was discovered in 1969 at Moshchevaya Barka, in the Caucasus, in a tomb in the Elbruz Mountains. A piece of paper manuscript in Chinese was with it. (Hermitage Museum, Leningrad)

In Turkey, silk forms a large part of the textile industry. The cocoon market at Bursa is especially famous, and is held every year in June.

Silk fabric with the famous design showing the bowman on horseback. Tang dynasty (AD 618 – 907).

Damask silk fabric with design of trees, sheep and birds in pairs, discovered at Turfan. 5th – 6th century.

abolition of private weaving enterprises to the advantage of the imperial workshops, or gynaeceums, which then had the monopoly of purchasing and weaving.

It was gradually at this time, in the mid-6th century, that an event occurred that would change the situation in which the Byzantine Empire was dependent on Persia under the Sassanids. Let us see how Procopius of Caesarea (died AD 562) recounts the situation:

'At about this time, certain monks from India, knowing with what zeal the emperor Justinian endeavoured to prevent the Romans from buying silk from the Persians, came to visit the sovereign and promised him that they would undertake the manufacture of silk, in order to avoid the future purchase of this merchandise by the Romans from the Persians, their enemies or from any other race. They had, they said, spent a certain time in a country named Serinda, situated over numerous Indian tribes, and had examined with great care by what means it might be possible to manufacture silk in the land of the Romans. As the emperor plied them with questions, and asked them whether they were indeed telling the truth, the monks explained that silk was produced by certain worms, which had been taught the art by nature and which had been obliged by her to work. They added that it was impossible to bring (the worms) from Serinda, but that it was very easy and straightforward to produce them; that the seed of the worms was composed of a multitude of eggs; that, long after they had been laid, people covered the eggs with dung and, allowing them to grow warm over a suitable period of time, brought about the birth of the animals. On hearing this, the emperor promised these men great favours and engaged them to confirm their reports by practice. They thus returned to Serinda and brought back eggs from there to Byzantium, they succeeded in transforming them into worms in the manner described, and fed (these worms) on mulberry leaves; and since then the

Romans have begun to make silk.' (*War of the Goths,* IV, 17). It is not known where the monks came from, nor what their religion was. According to Theophanus of Byzantium (c. AD 750 – 817), who tells the same story, sericulture was introduced by a Persian who came from the country of the Seres. In fact, this episode had no immediate effect. The Persian monopoly of silk lasted for some time yet. But, in the reign of Justin II (AD 567 – 578), thanks to the mission undertaken by the Sogdian merchant Maniakh, who had been sent to Byzantium by the empire of the eastern Turks who had just become established in Upper Asia, a new silk road was opened up to the north of the Caspian Sea and along the northern coast of the Black Sea. From that time on, the role of the Sogdians in the trading of silk and other products took on a great importance, the equivalent of that of the Greeks or Jews at the start of the Christian era.

The final stage in the art and craft of silk production was not reached until five centuries later, at the time of the Crusades, when Roger II, King of Sicily, deported weavers and women embroiderers to Palermo in the course of raids on Thebes, Athens and Corinth in 1146. And a further century would pass before sericulture passed from Sicily to Italy, first to Lucca, then to Venice and Florence.

In Turkey, silkworm-breeding is often a family activity. Here, the members of a family pick the cocoons from mulberry branches. Their technique of breeding is rather different from that customary in China.

The structure of different fabrics analysed under the microscope: above, a fragment of ancient silk (left) and a modern piece; below, a piece of crêpe de Chine (left) and a portion of Khotan silk.

Once the mulberry leaves have been picked, they are carried by donkey to the breeding-house.

35

THE CALL OF THE WEST

ALONG THE GREAT WALL OF CHINA

The departure point for travellers making their way to the countries of the West, a way followed equally by merchants and Buddhist pilgrims, was the Chinese capital, more precisely, one of the two capitals – that of the West, Changan. The present city of Xian (Sian), in the province of Shaanxi, is built on the site of the Changan of the Tang dynasty, and still preserves some traces of the period, whether restored or, more commonly, reconstructed.

A description of the city under the Tang has come down to us from the writings of the traveller Ibn-Wahad, in about AD 815, and recorded a century later by Abu Zaid:

'The town was very great, and its population extremely numerous. It was divided into two vast halves separated by a long, broad track. The emperor, his ministers, his guard, the supreme judge, the eunuchs, and all those who belonged to the imperial household, lived in the eastern part of the city. The ordinary population could not communicate with them and were not admitted to the places there, watered by many canals whose banks were planted with trees and decorated with sumptuous residences. The western part of the town was inhabited by the ordinary people and the merchants. They had great squares there and markets for the necessities of life. At daybreak, officers of the royal household would be seen there, together with purveyors and the servants of the courtiers. They came to this part of the town to visit the markets and the merchants' dwellings in order to buy all that they wanted, and they did not return until the following morning.'

There are a number of monuments which have survived from this period, in particular, the Great Pagoda of the Wild Goose, Dayan Ta, where the pilgrim Xuanzang (AD 602 – 664) had placed the Buddhist writings that he had brought from India. The Little Pagoda of the Wild Goose, Xiaoyan Ta, was built a little later, towards the end of the 7th century, by Empress Wu Zetian, as well as the Great Mosque, Qingzhenszi, dating from AD 742, in the Forest of the Steles, where over 1000 steles are preserved, and several temples. In its Chinese sector, the Silk Road was protected by the Great Wall of China, from the period of the Han down to the Ming, with the Wall itself built as a line of fortifications to prevent the incursion of nomadic tribes. It more or less succeeded in this aim, depending on the particular period.

The road that leads towards the western lands initially proceeds up the valley of the Wei. The length of the route to Central Asia and India, traces remain of Buddhist worship, which was made wherever sanctuary caves were set up. The best known of these, to the east of Changan itself, are those of Longmen, near Luoyang, the other capital, and of Yungang, near Datong, the ancient capital of the Northern Wei dynasty. In each case, the caves were dug out and sculpted at the exact period of the Wei dynasty, in the 5th century. On the Silk Road, as it makes its way to Central Asia, one of the most famous locations of Buddhist caves is that of Maijishan, near Tianshui in the valley of the Wei (province of Gansu), where there are over 190 caves with wall paintings and sculptures. Further west, not far from Lanzhou, and in an unusual site, are the caves of Binglingsi.

On leaving Lanzhou, the road takes a north-westerly direction, in what is traditionally known as the Hexi or Gansu Corridor, where it is locked between

the chain of the Qilian Mountains to the south and the Gobi Desert to the north. Under the Earlier Han, at the beginning of the 1st century BC, four commanderies were founded in this corridor, those of Wuwei, Zhangye, Jiuquan and Dunhuang. This occurred when the territories here were annexed as a result of the campaigns of General Huo Qubing. A line of defences linked with the two gateways to Yumen and Yang, and organised around the four garrisons, was set up to ensure freedom of passage. A rampart was built up to the gateways. All the caravan trade to the West or from the East had to pass along the Corridor.

Wuwei, which was known in the Tang period as Liangzhou, was the meeting-place of merchants from all the 'western districts' from the time when Xuangzang stayed there. It was there that all people entering or leaving Chinese territory were checked. When Xuangzang was dissuaded from leaving without permission, he decided to depart secretly.

A little to one side of the present road, the site of Karakhoto (the Black Town), located on the Edsengol river and mentioned by Marco Polo under the name of Edzina, was then on the road to Karakorum, which was the Mongol capital in the 13th century, before Kubilai transferred it to Khanbalik (Peking). As a Tangut city, reached from Ganzhou after twelve days on horseback, Karakhoto was the final staging post before entering the Gobi Desert. According to Marco Polo, it was not a trading town. Camels and livestock were plentiful there, and the city's falcons were famous.

Excavations made in 1974 in the mausoleum of the First Emperor of China, Qin Shi Huangdi, not far from Xian, revealed an army of almost seven thousand terracotta soldiers guarding his tomb.

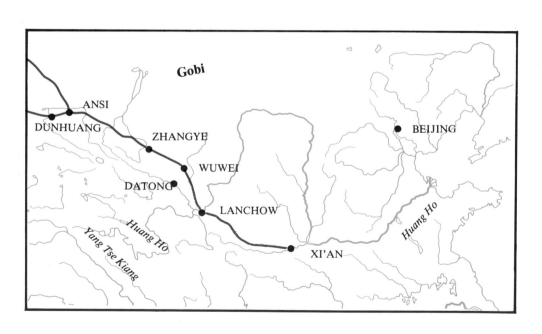

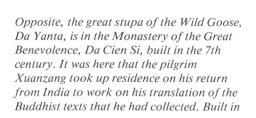

Opposite, the great stupa of the Wild Goose, Da Yanta, is in the Monastery of the Great Benevolence, Da Cien Si, built in the 7th century. It was here that the pilgrim Xuanzang took up residence on his return from India to work on his translation of the Buddhist texts that he had collected. Built in AD *652, the stupa, where the works were deposited, originally had five floors. When restored in the 8th century, two more floors were added. It was partially destroyed by fire in the 9th century, and was not rebuilt and restored until the 16th century.*

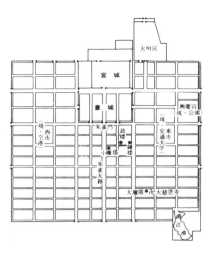

Like most ancient Chinese cities, Changan was built in the form of a square. The plan above re-creates the capital of the East during the Tang dynasty. The great stupa of the Wild Goose is situated to the south-east of the Imperial Palace.

The great mosque of Changan, Qingzhensi, was founded under the Tang in AD 742, but the present buildings date only from the end of the 14th century. The minaret is typically Chinese in style.

Mr Zuo's water wheels

On our journey, we came across several watermills, remarkable for their simplicity, like all things devised by the Chinese. In these mills, the upper millstone is stationary, and it is the lower one which turns by means of a single wheel, moved by a stream of water. To operate these mills, which are sometimes large in size, only a very small amount of water is necessary, for it falls on to the wheel as a cascade from a height of at least twenty feet.

R.-E. Huc, *Memoirs of a Journey to Tartary and Tibet*.

These water wheels, or norias, 18 metres in diameter, are used to pump water from the Yellow River to irrigate the crops. Their origin is uncertain, but the tale is told of how one Zuo Zondao, a local tribal leader, first put them to use. This is why they are known as 'Mr Zuo's water wheels'.

The Yellow River

The Yellow River rises in the Bayan Khara mountain chain, in the province of Qinghai. There are many legends about it. In its upper course, it waters the region of Lanzhou. A hundred kilometres west of this town, beside the Yellow River, where they are reached by boat, are the caves of Binglingsi (opposite).

Their archaeological discovery is relatively recent, as they had been 'forgotten' until 1952. Known under the Tang as Lingyansi, Monastery of the Supernatural Cliff, they received their present name much later.

The caves of Binglingsi

Binglingsi, whose name is simply a transcription of the Tibetan, meaning The Ten Thousand Buddhas, was already famous in the Tang dynasty. One hundred and ninety three caves or recesses are here, with the oldest dating back to the time of the Western Qin (AD 365 – 431), at the beginning of the 5th century. Arranged in three groups, the most important and interesting caves are in the group known as the 'Monastery of Down Below'. About ten caves or recesses date from the Wei, around a hundred from the Tang, and six from the Ming (1368 – 1644). In cave No. 80 of the Wei period, there is an inscription in the side of the cliff dating from AD 520 which mentions the vow made by the benefactor who had the cave dug and decorated: 'Cao Ziyuan had a cave built for the benefit of His Majesty the Emperor, his officers, his many functionaries and his people, and for that of his ancestors for seven generations. May his father and mother and his relations be born anew in the Paradise of the West and may all categories of beings themselves know happiness'.

The Binglingsi caves were restored and renovated in several stages. Two great statues of Buddha had been sculpted here, with the larger dating from the Tang period and measuring 27 metres high. Its upper portion is in stone, whereas the lower is sculpted in clay.

The Buddhist pantheon

The caves were originally known under the name of the Caves of Tangshu, this being a transcription of their name in a Tibetan dialect that means Caves of the Demons. Buddhism began to be practised under the Jin dynasty, in the 4th century, according to the *Fayuan Zhulin,* a Buddhist encyclopaedia of the 7th century written by the monk Daoshi (died AD 683): 'At the beginning of the Jin dynasty, the monastery of the valley of Tangshu was founded in the prefecture of the (Yellow) River. It is fifty *li* northwest of Hezhou. If you cross the ford of Fengli and if you climb the pass of Changyi, you will see to the south the famous Mountains of the Heaped Stones. This is the highest point, where

Above, in cave 68, a statue of the bodhisattva Avalokitesvara, or Guanyin, with eleven heads and eight arms, of the Ming dynasty, stands out on the painted wall.

Above right: Cave 169 is a natural cave, set up in AD 420, as indicated by the only inscription which remains. Above, right, three statues of the Buddha standing, in a style influenced by Central Asia and probably dating from the period of the cave's establishment, around the 5th century.

Yu the Great directed the course (of the Yellow River). All the peaks rise up in the most extraordinary shapes, looking like precious stupas or many-storeyed pavilions. Pines and cypresses show up on the summits, and reds and greens decorate the peaks. If this was not thanks to the magic powers of nature, how could such a beauty exist? Walking twenty *li* southwards, you come to this ravine. The mountain has been dug out, and caves have been established, their steps descending down to the water ... To the south there is a stone gate, on the bank of the River ...'

The Binglingsi caves are not only embellished with statues, but are also decorated with paintings. Cave 172 has its walls covered with repeated portrayals of small seated Buddhas. The figures all have different positions and their gestures, mudra, are also sketched differently, but following a strict code.

Above, in cave 172, a vajra bearer, jinghang lishi, a guardian and protector god habitually placed near the entrance.

49

The 'military horses' of Gansu

The 'military horses' that are still bred today near Shandan are a cross between the Mongol horses, which were small but sturdy, and the larger Kazakh horses.

At Leitai, near Wuwei, in the Hexi Corridor, bronze horses were discovered in 1969, dating from the Later Han (AD 25 – 220). One of these is the famous galloping horse with one foot on a swallow. There were also horsemen, chariots, etc.

The minorities of the Hexi Corridor

The Great Wall of China is the most absolute example of a frontier in history. 'Beyond the Wall, it's theirs; this side of the Wall, it's ours.' However, in the lives of men and the destiny of dynasties, the Great Wall simply established the extent of an adjacent area ... The concept of a frontier could not be realised, for one did not encounter two completely different societies. From the Neolithic age to the 20th century, there has always been some tilled land in Mongolia, and later, nomadic life was affected by commerce. Apart from the corn and millet grown on a small scale in Mongolia, the nomads had to import their crops from China. For the nomad, it was not really a necessity, but nor was it a luxury. The nomads could well have adjusted to a diet of meat, milk, and dairy products, but

The Great Wall of China, of which only traces remain here, was built to protect the Chinese against the raids of the Xiongnu. It thus divided the crop-growers from the stock-breeders, the settled peoples from the nomadic tribes, two kinds of contrasting cultures. Even so, if the Wall was an obstacle, it also served as a trading point.

The regions flanking the Great Wall are peopled by various non-Chinese ethnic groups who today live in autonomous districts. They include Mongols, Tibetans, Dongxiang, Baoan, Yugu, etc.

grain helped to preserve the value of their flocks. Even a castrated sheep regularly provided wool. Kill a sheep, and you liquidate and consume its capital, so putting an end to its productivity.

OWEN LATTIMORE, *Nomads and Commissars*

The Yugu, nomadic stock-breeders

They dress themselves in sable skins. In summer they wear them with the fur side outside, in winter with the fur inside. They have all kinds of other furs which they wear in the same manner. Their bedding and hangings are of furs and sheepskins. Their sewing-thread is made of tendons and their cord of sheep gut. For them, a steel needle is an object of luxury, costing much. For a single needle, they will give you a sheep. They own great herds of wild ponies, and of camels and sheep. They feed on gazelles, on wild ponies and on wild camels, and on game that is very abundant in their land.

SAYYID ALI-AKBER KHITAYI, *Treatise on China*

Peoples of different ethnic groups inhabit the Hexi Corridor. One of the non-Chinese minorities who live in the south of Jiuquan in the Qilian Mountains are the Yugu. They are a people that breed deer and sheep. They now live in an autonomous district, with traditions that are both Tibetan, Uigur and Mongol.

The barbarian tent

It is the tent of a barbarian family;
Year after year, it is still among the grass.
In summer the felt hangings are stretched out;
In winter skin furs are hung.
Their language can be scarcely understood.
Form morning to morning they graze their horses on the untilled hills ...

SIR AUREL STEIN, *Dunhuang*, ms 2607

Camels can travel nearly 40 kilometres a day, which is approximately the distance between one oasis and the next.

On page spread overleaf: The Qilian Mountains, sometimes called the Nanshan, Mountains of the South, border the Hexi Corridor to the south. They extend for some 800 kilometres and are 4000 metres high at their peak.

55

The Monastery of the Sleeping Buddha

The Monastery of the Great Buddha, Dafosi, or of the Sleeping Buddha, Shuifosi, was built in 1098, in the Tang dynasty of the Xi Xia. It was originally known as the Monastery of the Tathagatha Kasyapa, Jiaye Rulai Si. It changed its name under the Ming, but was still known under its popular name of Dafosi or Shuifosi.

These monasteries house a very great number of idols, some of which are ten paces high. Some are of wood, some of clay, some of stone and some of bronze, all covered in gold and wondrously worked. But there are some that are not so big and some that are small. The big idols lie with several other small idols standing round them, like disciples that humbly make obeisance. The big idols are moreover much more frequently worshipped than the small ones.

MARCO POLO,
Description of the World

The western limit of the Great Wall of the Ming was frequently moved over the ages by way of an extension of Chinese jurisdiction. Reaching as far as Lobnor under the Han, it did not go beyond Gansu in the time of the Ming. The fort that remains as Jiayuguan was built in 1372. Abandoned soon after, it was restored at the beginning of the 16th century. The fortress is square in shape. Two gates give access to it, one from the east and the other from the west. It is

Opposite: The fortress of Jiayuguan (opposite), 40 kilometres west of Jiuquan, was built in 1372. Four hundred soldiers were permanently billeted there.

surrounded by 10-metre-high defence walls, built of packed earth covered in brick. Not far from the western gate there is an inscription which was engraved in four characters on a stone stele in 1809: 'The most important passage in the empire'. This inscription echoes the one by the fortress at Shanhaiguan, at the other end of the Great Wall.

The extreme point of the territory that was properly that of the Chinese in the west was Dunhuang (or Shazhou, the Prefecture of the Sands), the outermost of the four commanderies founded under the Han, and the final stage before the hazards of the desert routes. The pilgrim Faxian halted here, as did both Xuanzang and Marco Polo. The latter, who calls it Saciu, observed an active religious observance on the part of the 'idolaters', that is, the Buddhists: 'They have many caves and monasteries, which are all full of idols of all kinds to which rich sacrifices are made, as well as great honour and great obeisance'. Marco Polo also describes a ritual offering of sheep: 'And you must know that all the men who have children feed a sheep each year in honour of the idols. At the beginning of the year, or on the feastday of the idol, those fathers who have fed the sheep lead it together with their child before the idol, and making great obeisance before it, hold a festival for the idol, they and their children'.

In about 1035, in the first half of the 11th century, the region of Dunhuang was conquered by the Tangut, a people of Tibetan origin, who founded a dynasty known as the Western Xia, Xi Xia (1032 – 1227), in the area of the present provinces of Gansu and

DUNHUANG, THE SACRED OASIS

Ningxia. The Chinese dynasty of the Song were unable to resist the Tangut, and they were only finally dominated with the help of the Mongols. The benefactor of the painting in cave 409, right, shown dressed in a Chinese-style robe and attended by several servants, is probably one of the kings of the Xi Xia.

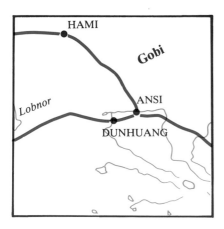

This religious practice had been engaged for a long time, and Dunhuang was one of the great places for Chinese Buddhist worship, as testified by the Caves of the Thousand Buddhas, of which the most famous are the caves of Mogao, about 25 kilometres south-east of the present town. Another smaller group, called the Caves of the Thousand Buddhas of the West, are some 35 kilometres west of Dunhuang. This kind of sanctuary cave is really of Indian origin, with the 'fashion' having travelled from Ajanta across the Buddhist route via Bamiyan and Turkistan to the very centre of China.

The site at Mogao numbers almost five hundred painted caves and recesses decorated with sculptures (or more precisely carved statues). According to tradition, the first cave is said to have been dug out and established towards the middle of the 4th century, in 366 or 353 BC. Gradually, other caves were excavated and decorated, both large and small, from the time of the Northern Wei to that of the Yuan. The paintings in some of the caves were sometimes covered with another picture at a later period.

The complex of caves has been excavated from a cliff that backs on to a sand-covered mountain, The Mountain of the Singing Sands, Mingsha Shan. Opposite the caves, across the river, there is another mountain, the Mountain of Three Dangers, Sanwei Shan. A description of the site has come down to us in a manuscript discovered at Dunhuang and probably written in the 9th century: 'To the south of the town of Shazhou, at a distance of twenty-five *li*, are the caves of Mogao. The road there passes through a desert of stones and along the side of a mountain, and when you arrive, there is an abrupt descent to the valley. To the

east are the Mountains of the Three Dangers. To the west, the Mountains of the Singing Sands. Between the two there flows from the south a river called the Source of the Caves, Dangquan. There are numerous temples and monasteries there. There are also some huge bells. At the two ends of this valley, to the north and south, there are the Temples of the Celestial King, Tianwang, as well as the sanctuaries of gods. The walls are painted in honour of the king of Tibet and his retinue. Over the whole of the western side of the mountain, for a distance of two *li* from north to south, huge, high caves have been dug out and sculpted. They contain modelled or painted Buddhist images. For each cave, the total expenditure has been considerable. Before them, pavilions of several storeys have been built. There is a room containing a great Buddha, one hundred and sixty feet high. The small recesses are innumerable. All the caves are linked by balus-

Opposite: The Mogao caves are the Mountains of the Three Dangers, Sanwei Shan, so named because of their three peaks. They have been described since ancient times in the Book of Writings, Shujing. The tireless sovereign, Yu the Great, in the third millennium BC, is said to have directed the course of the Black River to the Mountains of the Three Dangers.

A great statue of Buddha, 33 metres high, and erected in AD 695, backs on to the cliff. It has been protected by a nine-storey pavilion, whose summit overhangs the top of the escarpment.

trades which are for pilgrimages and visits. On the mountain, to the south, there is a place where the bodhisattva Guanyin once appeared. When people of the district come to these places, they arrive and return on foot. This is a sign of veneration. The Mountains of the Singing Sands are ten *li* from the town. From east to west, they stretch for eighty *li,* and from north to south, forty *li.* The highest points ascend to five hundred feet. They are entirely covered in sand. The spirits of these mountains are strange. The summits are steep. In the middle there is a hole of water which the sand has not been able to cover. At the height of the summer, a singing comes from the sands. The people and horses who gather here can hear the sound for scores of *li.* According to custom, on the *duanwu* (fifth day of the fifth month), the boys and girls of the town climb the highest peaks and tumble together down to the bottom. This causes a rumbling from the sand

like that of thunder. And when you look (at the mountains) at daybreak, they are as steep as before. Formerly, the Singing Sands were called the Supernatural Sands, and people made sacrifices to them' (*Dunhuang Lu,* Notes on Dunhuang, Sir Aurel Stein ms 5448).

The same manuscript also describes the sites near Dunhuang, such as the Spring of Ershi, to the east of the town, which is said to have appeared at the time of the military expedition of General Li Guangli, the general of Ershi, to the Wusun. Suffering from thirst, he pierced the side of the mountain with his sword, and a spring came forth. Its outflow depended on the thirst of those who drank, and its waters were abundant if they were numerous, but scarce if they were few.

The Gate of Yang, Yangguan, one of the outposts that gave access to the routes to Turkistan, is also mentioned in this manuscript, and its origin established: 'To the west of the town is the Gate of Yang, which is like the ancient Gate of Jade, Yumenguan. It derives its name from the occasion when the prefect Yang Ming opposed the order of arrest placed on him and fled through this gate. As a result, people called it the Gate of Yang. It established a link with the town of Shanshan. But the dangerous passes and the absence of water and vegetation meant that people would not venture there. As a result, this gate was moved to the east of the town.'

Whereas the Gate of Yang opened the route to the south, the other gate, the Gate of Jade, Yumenguan, opened the route to the north, to Hami. The passage of Yumenguan had somewhat concerned Xuanzang on his departure. 'Fifty *li* from here, going to the north, you come to the Hulu river whose lower course is broad but whose upper course very narrow. Its currents turn constantly and flow so violently that it cannot be crossed by boat. It was after the broadest part that the Gate of Jade was set up, though which you were obliged to pass and which is the western frontier. To the north-west, beyond this gate, there are five signal towers where the sentinels keep their watch. The towers are a hundred *li* from one another. In the interval between them, there is neither grass nor pastureland. Beyond these five towers stretch the Mojiayan (Gobi) desert and the frontiers of the Yiwu kingdom (Hami)' (Huili and Yanzong, *Biography of Xuanzang,* 1).

Another manuscript, also discovered in the Dunhuang caves, is a monograph on Shazhou, written and copied in the 8th century. It tells us what then remained of the Great Wall on the territory of Dunhuang: 'The old Great Wall is eight feet high (2.40 metres), ten feet broad at the base, and four feet at the top. It is sixty-three *li* north of the town. To the east, it extends to the signal tower Jieting (Stage of the Ladder), at a distance of one hundred and eighty *li,* where you enter the territory of the district of Changle, at Guadzhou. To the west, it runs to the signal tower Quze (Lake of Waves), two hundred and twelve *li* distant, where you enter straight into the desert which borders the territory of Shicheng (Loulan)' (*Shazhou Dufu Tujing,* Pelliot Chinese ms 2005).

This same manuscript, among other details, gives the names of the staging posts on the territory of Dunhuang. There were then nineteen posts deployed on three routes leading to Guazhou (Anxi) or Yiwu (Hami).

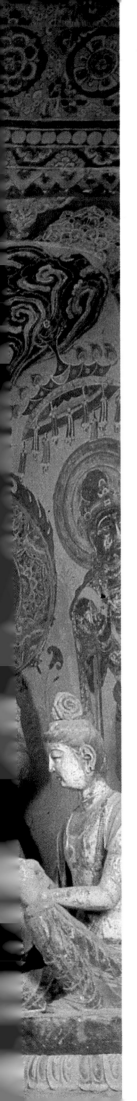

The Buddhist sculptures

The caves of Mogao date from the second year *jianyuan* of the Early Qin (AD 366). The monk Luocun, pure and humble in nature, in conformity with his beliefs, ranged the forests and the plains, his pilgrim's staff in his hand. In walking, he came to this mountain and suddenly saw a golden light formed of a thousand Buddhas ... He dug out a cave. Next, the master of *dhyana*, Faliang, came here from the east. And, beside the cave of the master (Luo-)cun, he likewise set up a building. The erection of sacred buildings began with these two monks.

Text on a stele erected at Dunhuang in 698.

On the eastern wall of cave 328 a recess has been hollowed out containing seven figures, statues sculpted under the Tang (page left). In the centre, the seated Buddha is preaching the Law. Standing next to him, one on each side, are his disciples Ananda and Kasyapa, together with two seated bodhisattva and two kneeling with offerings. The one on the left has disappeared, having been taken to the United States in 1924 by Langdon Warner.

In front of a wall painted with 'a thousand Buddhas', three statues, dating from the Sui dynasty (AD 581 – 618), decorate the north wall of cave 427. Buddha is preaching the Law, accompanied by two bodhisattva. The tallest statue is 4.25 metres high (above right).

Page spread overleaf: Cave 220, completed at the beginning of the Tang period, more exactly in AD 642, and restored several times since, is decorated on its north wall with a huge paradise scene by Bhasajyaguru, Yaoshi, the Master of the Cures. At the foot of the painting is an orchestra and two girl dancers, reminding us that the music of Kucha and Central Asia was very popular at that time, as were the 'barbarian' dancing girls and their revolving dances.

The wall paintings

Domed cellings are fairly rare in the Dunhuang caves. They are most easily seen in the caves of the Kucha region, for example at Kizil. Cave 272 (right) is one of the most ancient to have such a ceiling. It probably dates from the beginning of the 5th century.

One day when he had gone to seek fruit, he encountered on his way a tigress suckling her cubs. When the tigress had finished, she was very exhausted and had nothing to eat. Crazy with hunger, she was about to return and eat her own young. Seeing this, the bodhisattva was moved with pity. He thought with compassion on all living beings who endure infinite suffering during their stay in the world ...

LIUDU JIJING

The ceiling of the main chamber of cave 285 (right), dating from the Western Wei (AD 535 – 556), has a centre showing the story of Fuxi and Nugua, the creators of human beings, surrounded by apsara and various other gods.

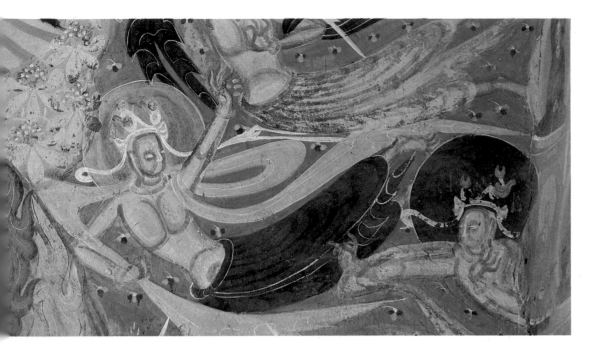

The flying goddesses of apsara, feitian, make a decorative motif originating from the 'Regions of the West', and frequently found in the Dunhuang cave paintings. Tang Hou, who lived in the Yuan dynasty (1271 – 1368), wrote about the apsara in his 'Mirror of Painting', Huajian: 'They fly like silkworms spitting threads of silk, like spring clouds floating in the sky, like water flowing over the ground'. Left: Apsara in cave 288, dating from the Western Wei (AD 535 – 556). Below, apsara in cave 290, dating from the Northern Zhou (AD 557 – 581).

The former lives of the Buddha, jataka, are frequently illustrated in the Dunhuang cave paintings. Here (above) one can easily make out part of the story of the hungry tigress who had nothing to eat and who was about to devour her cubs when the Buddha, in a former life, offered her his own body out of pity.

Page spread overleaf: The whole upper section of the walls in cave 61 is devoted to paintings of benefactors. It portrays a virtual procession consisting solely of feminine figures. The majority are designated by their title, inscribed in a scroll. Several titles have now been erased or are illegible, but one can still identify Uigur and Khotan princesses linked by marriage to the reigning Dunhuang family.

The statue of Buddha lying, that is, entering nirvana, in cave 81 dates from the middle of the Tang dynasty. It was constructed out of stone and clay. The stone came from the excavation, and was used to form the base of the statue, with the sculpting worked in clay.

He (Li Taipin) found a spot to carve, but he had no one to do it with him. So, at the cost of a thousand pounds of gold, he hired workmen. The walls rose in their hundreds. The hammer blows deafened the valley, and the carrying of stone echoed in the mountain. A statue of the Buddha in nirvana was fashioned, as well as statues of the bodhisattva Cintamanicakra and Amoghapasa. Portraits were painted of the bodhisattva Samantabhadra and Manjusri, of the Master of the Cures of the East and of the Pure Land of the West, of Avalokitesvara 'of the thousand hands and thousand eyes', of the births of Maitreya, Cintamanicakra and Amogha-pasa. For the thousand pictures of the thousand Buddhas of the period itself, models were first made from clay, then coloured. The wall was widely cleared of stone and the golden face appeared, imposing.

Inscription on the stele erected in AD 776 before the Cave of the Sleeping Buddha.

Preceding page spread: Several of the Dunhuang caves are decorated almost entirely with little painted Buddhas, especially in the later periods of the Xi Xia or the Yuan (11th – 14th centuries) and often when the pictures were restored or repainted. The centre of the ceiling in cave 392, dating from the beginning of the Tang period and restored in the 10th century, presents a pattern of apsara and wavy clouds.

THE TAKLA MAKAN DESERT

The first stage on the southern route of the Takla Makan Desert was formerly Loulan (or Shanshan) beside Lake Lobnor. The name and location of the capital of this ancient kingdom have been the subject of many disagreements on the part of historians and archaeologists.

The pilgrim Faxian (born about AD 340) stayed there for more than a month and told in his account of his journey, which had this place as its starting point, how it appeared to him that he had really left China. 'The kingdom of Shanshan is a mountainous and very uneven land. The earth is thin and barren. The customs and clothes of the inhabitants are coarse, and resemble those of the Han country. The sole difference is in their use of felt and fabrics ... From here on, all the kingdoms that you come across when travelling westwards are more or less like this one, only each kingdom has a barbarian tongue that is different'.

1. THE ROUTE OF THE KUNLUN MOUNTAINS

To the south-west of Lake Lobnor, on the present route, the oasis of Miran was probably deep inside the kingdom of Shanshan, but travellers' tales leave us little information to go on.

Farther west, the town of Cherchen has long been identified with the ancient city-state of Qiemo, mentioned in the History of the Han (*Hanshu*). The grape was harvested there, as were various kinds of fruit. The pilgrim Songyun (6th century) declared that, for his part: 'In this region, it does not rain, and water has been channelled to make the corn grow. (The inhabitants) do not know how to use oxen, nor ploughs for cultivating their fields. In this town are portrayals of the Buddha and a bodhisattva who do not have barbarian faces at all'.

The present route continues to the site of Endere, but passes to one side, that of Niya, which corresponds to the ancient city-state of Jingjue. It then reaches Keriya (Yutian). This is possibly the town that Marco Polo called Pem, that is to say Bima in Chinese, a town praised by its Buddhist pilgrims Songyun and Xuanyang because of a miraculous statue. 'In this town, you can see a statue of the Buddha shown standing. It is thirty feet high and is at once remarkable for the beauty of its outline and for the serious and severe expression of the figure. It works a multitude of miracles for those who call on the Buddha. If a man is sick and, according to the place where he suffers, a golden leaf is stuck on the statue, he will immediately he healed. The prayers and requests that are addressed to the statue are almost always crowned with success'.

Tradition tells how this statue, which was made at the time when the Buddha was still alive, had come from India, having been transported through the air.

A little to the east, Khotan (Hetian, formerly Yutian) has long been an important kingdom. In the 10th century, its sovereign, married to the daughter of a governor of Dunhuang, was even given the title of emperor. Faxian makes mention of Khotan in his account of his journey, as does Xuanzang. The origin of the town of Khotan is swathed in Buddhist mythology, since it is said to have been founded by a god, Vaisravana (Bishamen). The traditional tale found in

Opposite: The routes across the Takla Makan Desert were feared by travellers, who vied with one another to tell how the only landmarks for finding one's way were the bones of travellers before them or of dead animals.

People tell as an accepted matter that in the said desert there live a number of spirits who produce great and surprising illusions on travellers in order to cause them to perish. And it is true that when you ride at night through this desert, and one or other of the merchants falls behind, and is separated from his companions in order to sleep or for some other reason, if the company disappears behind a hill or mountain, when he seeks to rejoin his companions, it often happens that you can hear evil spirits talking in the air in a way that resembles that of his companions. For ofttimes they call him by name, and ofttimes, causing him to believe that they are his companions, he follows these voices and leaves the right road. In such a manner, he never rejoins his companions, and he is never found again, and no one has any news of him, for no one knows how to return to him. And finding themselves without food or drink, many travellers have died in past times, and been lost. Men hear the voices of spirits, and it appears to you many times that you hear many musical instruments sounding in the air, especially drums and the blows of weapons. Therefore those who wish to follow the path and pass over the desert must take great care of themselves so as not to be separated from their friends for any reason, and must go with great prudence, hanging bells round the necks of their horses and animals in order to hear them continuously, in such a way that they do not fall asleep or wander from the track'.

MARCO POLO, *Description of the World*

Tibetan texts is different from that of Xuanzang, but the two accounts agree on the fact that Khotan resulted from a melding of exiles from India and China.

Xuanzang tells how the first king ensured his succession. 'He was ninety years old, and he had come to an extreme old age without having any heir. Fearing that his family would die out, he went to the temple of the god Bushamen (Vaisravan), and fervently begged him to give him an heir. Suddenly the head of the statue opened above the forehead, and a young boy came out. The king took him and returned to his palace . . .'

Khotan has always been famous for its jade. 'There is a river there which contains jade. At night, the local people observe the places where the reflection of the moon is strong and do not fail to find beautiful jade there' (*Tangshu*, History of the Tang, 221). The production of jade was already mentioned as occurring under the Han, and the attraction of the Chinese to the jade of Khotan was incessant. At the beginning of the 17th century, the Jesuit Beneditto Goës wrote of the significant traffic in jade which existed with the Chinese capital. 'They bring this marble to the king because of the great amount of money that the King of Cathay pays for it, believing that that is fitting for his royal dignity . . . They make many and various kinds of furniture from this marble, as well as vases, ornaments of apparel and belts, on which they engrave leaves and flowers most clearly, which indeed embellish the work and make it more majestic.'

Farther again to the west are the oases of Karghalik (Yecheng) and Yarkand (Suoju). From Karghalik, to the south, one fork of the road makes its way to

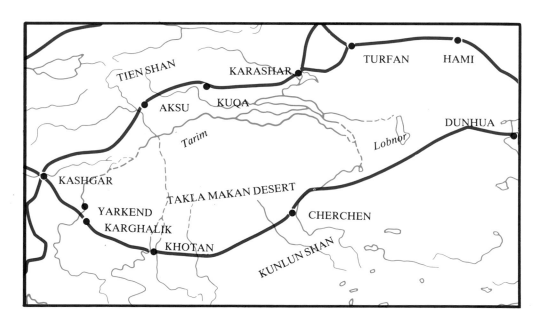

Laak across the Kunlun Mountains and the Karakorum Chain. It was in these mountains that the Suspended Paths mentioned in the *History of the Han* were located. Farther north, Yarkand is mentioned by Marco Polo, who noticed a singular feature, so singular, indeed, that it is all the less credible. 'The people are good workmen. They mostly have one big foot and the other very small, but notwithstanding this they walk very well.'

From Yarkand, one can continue westwards to Taskkurgan, as Faxian appears to have done, or towards the north-west to Kashgar, where the road links up with the Northern Takla Makan route.

In praise of the camel

And I tell you that this desert is so long, according to what is said, that it takes a year to reach the end of it. Across it, where it is less broad, you toil for a month. Thus, in its length, it cannot be travelled, for you cannot take enough food. In its width, as has been said, you can walk for a month without ever finding a roof. It is all sandy mountains and plains, and also valleys, and there is nothing there to eat. But I tell you that, whoever has travelled for a day and a night, will find in winter water that is sweet to drink, but not enough for a great company, just what is needed for fifty to a hundred men and their animals, and no more. It is thus necessary to cross in a small company, no greater than fifty at once. And across the whole desert it is fitting for you to travel a day and a night before you find water to drink. Moreover, I tell you that in three or four places, you find bitter water, salty and harmful, whereas other places are good to drink, but nowhere abundantly. And there are about twenty-eight water places. There is no beast of any kind, nor any bird, for they would find nothing to eat.

MARCO POLO, *Description of the World*

Right, and in page spread overleaf: The arid wastes of the Takla Makan Desert were always dreaded by travellers. In the Uigur language, its name means 'the desert of irrevocable death'.

The camels

To the north-west of Qiemo (Cherchen), there are shifting sands for several hundred *li*. In the summer period, there are hot winds which are a disaster for travellers. When such a wind is about to rise, only the old camels know beforehand. They immediately begin to groan and, keeping together, bury their muzzles in the sand. People always take that as a warning and they, too, immediately cover their nose and mouth with blankets. The wind is sudden, and only lasts a short while, but if you take no protection, you can expect death.

History of the Northern Dynasties, Beishi, 97

The camel is an unusual domestic animal. He carries a saddle of flesh on his back. He runs rapidly over shifting sands. He shows his worth in dangerous places. He has a secret knowledge of springs. His knowing is truly subtle!

GUO PU, 3rd century, *In Praise of the Camel, Tuotuo Zan*

The ruins of Miran

The half-buried rooms and shelters which had housed the Tibetan garrison of the 8th and 9th centuries were quite sturdy in their shape and construction, but they proved to contain, in some parts, the most remarkable heaps of waste matter that it has ever been my lot to remove.

SIR AUREL STEIN,
On Ancient Central Asian Tracks

Miran, 85 kilometres north-east of Charklik, was a fortress of the kingdom of Shanshan from the time of the Early Han to the 4th century. The abandoned site was again occupied between the 7th and 9th centuries by the Tibetans, before disappearing again until the archaeologist Aurel Stein, at the beginning of the 20th century, published its manuscripts and paintings. In these one can see many foreign influences, such as Graeco-Roman, Mesopotamian or Indian.

Niya, ancient capital of the kingdom of Jingjue

The site of Niya, about 120 kilometres north of Minfeng, which now consists only of ruins, was formerly known under the Han as the kingdom of Jingjue. The city then numbered 480 families, or 3360 inhabitants of whom 500 were able to bear arms. The ruins of the dwellings still show a quite sophisticated type of construction, originally made of wood and clay mixed with reeds and sprigs of tamarisk.

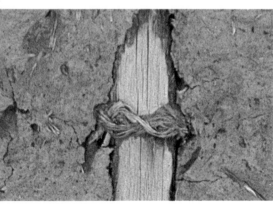

Opposite: Several mummified corpses have been discovered by archaeologists in the tombs of the oases in the Takla Makan Desert. This body of a woman (centre) was wrapped in a rough cloth. She was wearing a felt hat, two heron feathers decorated her hair, and on her feet were shoes of camel hide.

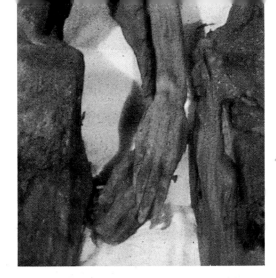

Here, the walls and all objects which could have been abandoned are now entirely worn away by erosion, although the massive pillars, whitened and split, are still standing, indicating the position of the original framework. But when I examined the floor of what seemed to have been a shed or a stable, I quickly noticed that it consisted of layers of heaped up refuse. Naturally, previous

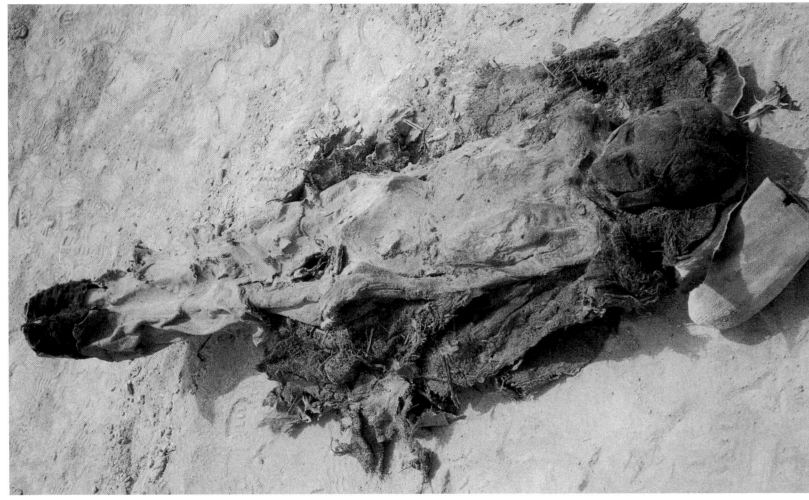

experience gave me sufficient cause to rummage in this unpleasant quarry, even though the strong odours given off by its contents, after seventeen centuries of being buried, were doubly taxing in the fresh easterly breeze which scattered a fine dust of dead microbes etc. into my eyes, throat and nose.

SIR AUREL STEIN, *On Ancient Central Asian Tracks*

The oasis of Khotan

Khotan, more than any other oases of the Takla Makan Desert, has a population that is 95% Uigur. The donkey is the most widespread animal used for transport within the town, and a simple cart can even be used as a taxi.

On page spread overleaf: At Yarkand, silkmaking is still a common activity. In the shade of the mulberry trees, women spin silk or sew bonnets.

95

The spread of Islam

Being questioned regarding the law that he observed, whether that of Moses, David or Mahomet, and regarding the direction in which he turned to pray to God, Beneditto replied that he was of the law of Jesus (whom they called *Isai)* and that he turned in all directions when praying, because it was certain that God was everywhere. This last reply provoked a great discussion between them, for they turn to the east to pray to their impostor. Finally they concluded that our law could also seem equally valid.

M. RICCI, N. TRIGAULT,
*History of the Christian Expedition
to the Kingdom of China*

Khotan, where Buddhism had at one time been important, passed to Islam towards the end of the 10th century. Since then, Moslem worship has remained widespread, whatever the political régime. Friday afternoon prayers at the Great Mosque bring together many faithful.

The greatest bazaar
on the southern route

In this country they make wine from the grape. There is also a purple wine, and another of a blue colour. I do not know what they are made from, but their taste is very agreeable. The inhabitants eat rice dressed with honey, and millet cooked in cream. Their clothing is made of cloth and silk. They have gardens where they grow flowering trees. They worship spirits, especially the Buddha.

History of the Town of Khotan

Since the fall of their empire in Mongolia in the 10th century, the Uigur have dispersed to most of the oases in what is now Chinese Turkistan. Although originally a wild nomadic people of the steppes, they have gradually become a settled race.

The custom of this people is for women to wear drawers and short dresses tied with a belt. They climb up on horses and camels just like men. The dead are burned, their bones are gathered, they are then buried, and a chapel to the Buddha is erected over the grave. People who are in mourning shave their hair, and nick their faces as a sign of grief. When their hair has grown to a length of five inches, they resume their normal lives.

History of the Town of Khotan

The three rivers of jade

To the east of the town of Yutian (Khotan) is the River of White Jade, Baiyu He. To the west, is the River of Green Jade, Lüyu He. There is a third river, that of Black Jade, Heiyu He, also to the west of the town.

History of the Ming, Mingshi

Khotan, which has always been a leading commercial and trading centre, possesses what is undoubtedly the largest bazaar on the southern route through the Takla Makan Desert. Situated in the main street, it is still one of the most important scenes of activity and enjoyment in the city.

102

2. THE ROUTE OVER THE CELESTIAL MOUNTAINS

From Dunhuang and Tumenguan, on the northern route, the first staging post was at Hami (Yiwu under the Tang, Camul for Marco Polo). It was reached only after crossing a desert that was feared by travellers. Xuanzang, having left the Yumen Pass, followed the Great Wall as far as the fourth signal tower, then from there struck north-west into the desert formerly called River of Sand (Shahe) or Hillocks of the White Dragons. Xuanzang tells us nothing about Yiwu, but a manuscript text copied in 886, and discovered in the Dunhuang caves, informs us about some of the customs attributed to the inhabitants, who made their living in agriculture and commerce. 'Winter and summer, they eat griddle cakes. They have no cooking equipment. They have no cups, no bowls, no spoons, no chopsticks. When they are thirsty, they simply squat down and drink straight out of the ground' (Sir Aurel Stein ms 367).

Much later, Marco Polo described another custom of these people. 'If a stranger passing through the region comes to one of their houses to stay the night, the man of the house greatly rejoices and welcomes the visitor with great joy, and takes all the trouble in the world to please him. He orders his wife, daughters, sisters and other female relatives to do everything for the stranger better than they would do it for himself. He goes from his house, leaving his wife with the stranger, and sets off to see to his business, staying two or three days in the country. And from there he sends all that his guest wishes, but only for payment, and does not return home so long as the stranger is still there.'

The Uigurs, a people of nomadic origin whom the Chinese under the Tang linked with the Xiongnu, were subjects of the Turks (Tujue) before founding their own empire in the 8th century in what is now Mongolia. In the 10th century, some of their tribes regrouped in the region of Ganzhou (Zhangye) in Gansu and in Xizhou (Turfan) in Xinjiang. The state that they established in this part of the world was not conquered until the 13th century by the Mongols.

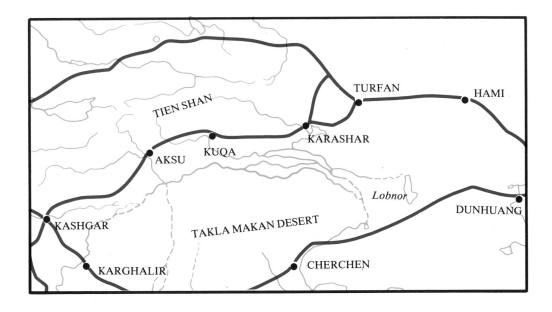

Continuing westwards, after Hami, the route comes out into the Turfan basin (the name is sometimes pronounced Turpan, in the Turkish manner), a broad depression that is for the most part situated below sea level. The great dryness and extremes of temperature are compensated by an irrigation system which is also found in Iran and whose origin is uncertain. It consists of *karez,* underground channels that link wells.

The ancient town of Jiaohe (Yarkhoto), to the west of the present town of Turfan, on a hill spur between two branches of the river, was the seat of the city-

Gaochang

*A few kilometres east of Turfan,
Gaochang, at the foot of the Flaming
Mountains, Huoyanshan, was the seat
of a prefecture established under the
Tang in AD 640. It had the name of
Xizhou, and was the Uigur capital from
the 9th century.*

*Opposite: The ruined town of
Gaochang, square in shape, had an area
of 1.5 square kilometres. The outer wall
is well preserved, but almost all the
brick buildings have been destroyed.
Some, however, have been restored.*

state of Jushi during the period of the Han. The Chinese seized it and founded a military colony a little to the east, at Gaochang (Kocho). This would become the administrative seat of the territory, alternating with Jiaohe, as much under Chinese domination as when independent. This lasted until the 14th century. The Turfan oases were an important point on the Silk Road, inasmuch as they opened up a route to the north that led to Beiting (Beshbalik, now Jimusa), where it joined the northern Tianshan route.

Xuanzang was received with great honour in Gaochang in 630. Buddhism was already well established there, as testified by the caves at Bezeklik or Toyuk. But when the Uigurs settled in the region in the 9th century, Manicheism was introduced.

To the west of the Turfan depression, at Toksun, the route makes its way towards Yanqi (Karashar), by Lake Bagrash. We are told that under the Tang both vines and millet were grown here and that fish and salt were traded. The inhabitants had their hair cut short and wore woollen clothing.

Further west still, the oasis at Kucha is still an important crossroads. To the west, the road leads on to Kashgar; to the north, across the Tien Shan Mountains, the route takes the traveller to Dzungaria; to the south-west, following the Tarim and the Khotan river, you reach Khotan. This diversity of routes is matched by a trade that is even more important. Under the Tang, the towns of Kucha, Karashar, Kashgar and Khotan had been ordered to raise taxes from merchants who had come from the western regions.

At Kucha, Xuanzang saw fine horses whose origin was said to go back to the mating of mares and dragons. But above all, he found about a hundred monasteries there and counted more than five thousand Buddhist religious, all adherents of the Little Vehicle. He also noted that the musicians there were particularly excellent. There were numerous statues of the Buddha and, once a year, these were taken by procession through the streets. Several remains of this intense Buddhist activity have been found near Kucha, and also at Kumtura, Subashi, Kizil and Duldur-Akur.

On its way further west, the route comes to Aksu, then to Kashgar (Shule), where it joins the southern route through the Takla Makan Desert. At Kashgar, Xuanzang noted that theft and deceit were commonplace. Moreover, when a child was born, he recounts, there was a custom of compressing its head to flatten it. The people were tattooed and had green eyes.

Marco Polo made only a brief stop at Kashgar. It was mainly a trading city, and a meeting-place for merchants. Finally, from Kashgar, apart from the routes that led eastwards, three directions could be taken: one to the north, towards Kirghizia and Lake Issik-Köl, another westwards, towards Tadzhikistan and Samarkand, and a third towards the south-west, through Tashkurgan, to Little Pamir and Balkh, or to Kashmir and India.

Jiaohe

The History of the Tang, *Tangshu,* gives us a brief description of the kingdom of Gaochang: 'It numbers in all twenty-one towns. The king has his capital in the town of Jiaohe which is none other than the former royal court (of the country) of Jushi at the time of the Han ... The kingdom has two thousand crack soldiers. The ground is fertile. Corn and crops produce two harvests a year. There is a plant there called *baidie* (no doubt cotton). Its flower is picked so that it can be woven to make cloth. The custom (of the inhabitants) is to plait their hair into a coil which hangs behind the head'.

To the north of the town, traces of a Buddhist monastery can be seen. Here, the remains of a stupa.

Left: A little to the west of Turfan, the ruins of the town of Jiaohe stand out on an island, a natural fortress, called also Yarkhoto or Idikut-Shari. Thirty days' walking is needed to reach it from Dunhuang.

The Turfan depression

A Chinese envoy to the Uigurs in 982, Wang Yande, made a number of observations on Turfan. 'In this country, it neither rains nor snows, and the heat is excessive. Every year, in the hottest season, the inhabitants retreat underground. Then birds gather in close groups on the banks of the river, and if any of them should chance to take flight, they are as it were burnt by the heat of the sun, so falling from on high through the air and breaking their wings. The houses are covered with a white earth ... There is a river which

The climate of Turfan is particularly dry, with only 16 mm of rain a year. The houses are of simple construction in crude brick, dried in the sun.

comes out of a mountain pass called Jinling. Its waters have been controlled in such a way that they surround the capital of the kingdom, water the fields and gardens, and turn the wheels of the mills.'

GAOCHANG XINGJI, *Account of a Journey to Gaochang*

In summer, the heat exceeds the average of 40°C. Shaded front gardens in which vines are grown enable a relative coolness to be conserved.

The most widespread means of transport in the oasis of Turfan is the horse-drawn cart or a rough cart harnessed to a donkey.

Page spread overleaf: The Caves of the Thousand Buddhas at Bezeklik, whose name in Turkish means 'decorated house', were excavated and established between the Sui and Yuan dynasties in the Murtuk ravine east of Turfan, at the foot of the Flaming Mountains. On the wall paintings that embellished the 57 existing caves, of which several were taken to Berlin by the archaeologists A. Grünwedel and A. von Le Coq, traces can be seen of a religious activity that was not only Buddhist but Manichean.

The Caves of the Thousand Buddhas of Bezeklik

The wall paintings of the caves of Bezeklik have been pillaged and mutilated more than once, often resulting from the fanaticism of certain Moslems. Cave 39 has a fragment of a painting executed in the Yuan dynasty. It probably illustrates a ceremony of condolence, with envoys from foreign countries. The presence of people of different races, dressed in different styles, reflects the high intensity of exchanges that took place over the Silk Road. The ruling for foreign delegations of China was extremely strict. Under the Tang, a special department was responsible for admitting foreigners to the court. Envoys were classified according to the status of their country of origin, and ranked as officers of the empire, with grades corresponding to the importance of the countries that they represented. Each envoy had a particular place for audiences at court. The gifts that were offered to the emperor were carefully examined and valued before being passed, according to their value, into imperial service, with the gifts of lesser value sent out to the prefectures.

Nanjiang, the railway of the 'southern Frontier'

Between Turfan and Korla, to the south of Karashar, the route through the Tien Shan Mountains has been duplicated by a recently built railway. This is the railway of the 'Southern Frontier', *Nanjiang*. The railway runs for 470 kilometres, and reaches a maximum altitude of 2900 metres, at which point a 6-kilometre-long tunnel has been constructed. On the other side of the mountain, the route comes out into the green Wulasitai valley, before again entering the Takla Makan Desert and so reaching Kucha.

Opposite and page spread overleaf: The southern route across the Takla Makan Desert had originally been the preferred one by Chinese travellers making for the West. Later, however, they came to prefer the northern route. Between Turfan and Karashar, two routes were possible. One was flat but through the desert. The other was mountainous, across the Tien Shan, but had the advantage of offering opportunities to find food and water.

The Kucha oasis

The kingdom of Quzhi (Kucha) is about a thousand *li* from east to west, and about six hundred *li* from south to north. The circumference of the capital is between seventeen and eighteen *li*. The soil is favourable for red millet and wheat. It moreover produces rice of the kind called *gentao,* grapes, pomegranates, and a great quantity of pears, plums, peaches and almonds. The ground contains gold mines, copper mines, iron mines, lead mines and tin mines. The climate is mild. The behaviour of the people is pure and honest. Their writing was taken from India, but with some modifications. The musicians of this land outshine those of other kingdoms by their talent on the flute and the guitar. The inhabitants

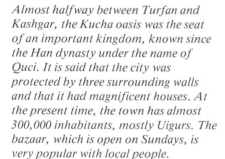

Almost halfway between Turfan and Kashgar, the Kucha oasis was the seat of an important kingdom, known since the Han dynasty under the name of Quci. It is said that the city was protected by three surrounding walls and that it had magnificent houses. At the present time, the town has almost 300,000 inhabitants, mostly Uigurs. The bazaar, which is open on Sundays, is very popular with local people.

Page spread overleaf: Kucha was noted for its music, more so than other 'western' regions. It was as a result of the Chinese conquest of this kingdom by General Lü Guang in 384 that the music of Kucha came to be appreciated at the Chinese court. This musical tradition is still maintained, even though the music itself has no doubt changed considerably. On the next page, a singer accompanies herself on the dotar.

wear clothing of silk brocade or coarse wool. They cut their hair short and wear bonnets. In trading, they use gold and silver pieces and little copper coins. The present king is of the Quzhi race. He has little prudence or ability, and allows himself to be dominated by powerful ministers. Normally, when a child is born, its head is flattened by being pressed with a board.

XUANZANG, XIYU JI, *Memoirs of Western Lands, 1*

Subashi:
The monasteries of
Zhaouli

Xuanzang, who was obliged
to stay over two months in the
region of Kucha because of the
harsh winter, visited the site of
Subashi, which he called the
'monasteries of Zhaohuli':
'Forty *li* to the north of the
town, at the foot of two
mountains separated only by a
river, are two monasteries called
by the same name of Zhaohuli,
and which are distinguished by
their eastern or western
position'. Richly decorated
statues of Buddha had been
placed here. The monks and the
faithful, Xuanzang tells us, were
pure and austere, and gave
evidence of the greatest zeal.

*The ruins of the old town of Subashi on
the banks of the Kucha river were
identified by Paul Pelliot on his arrival
here in 1907, as was the site of the
Loriot monasteries, formerly described
by Xuanzang. The Otani mission, in
1903, discovered just a pair of sandals
there. Numerous caves remain in the
nearby mountain. They are caves in the
form of a tunnel with recesses, which
doubtless served as places of meditation
for the monks.*

Yanshui: the Gorges of Salt Waters

The ancient route which led to Kashgar crosses the Gorges of Salt Waters, about ten kilometres north-west of Kucha. The route followed the bed of the dried-up river for most of the year, the soil of which is covered in salt. Salt is mentioned several times in travellers' tales, by both Marco Polo and by Wang Yande in the 10th century or Chang Chun in the 13th century. Wang Yande describes the salt in the mountains north of Beiting (Beshbalik), which people would come and collect wearing wooden-soled shoes. This was a necessary precaution, for leather soles would have been burnt. Chang Chun, south of Samarkand, noticed a salt spring whose water evaporated, leaving white salt on the surface of the soil. As for Marco Polo, he saw whole mountains of salt near Balkh, with the salt so hard that it could only be detached with an iron pickaxe, and in such abundance that there would have been enough for the whole world for all time.

The Caves of the Thousand Buddhas of Kizil

The Caves of the Thousand Buddhas of Kizil are located north-west of Kucha, on the north bank of the Muzart. Some 236 caves stretch for 2 kilometres from east to west, and were excavated between the 3rd and the 10th centuries. While some of the caves were used as sanctuaries, others seem to have been used for dwelling purposes. A library was also discovered there by the archaeologists Grünwedel and Le Coq, who unfortunately left behind manuscripts written on paper and birch bark. The most interesting or important caves were given individual names by the German archaeologists, according to their chief characteristics: Caves of the Musicians' Choir, of the Helmeted Horsemen, of the Peacocks, of the Monkey, of the Prayer Mill, of the ring-bearing Pigeons, and so on.

At left: Cave 38, arranged in the form of a tunnel, probably in the 3rd and 4th centuries, has been called the Cave of the Musicians' Choir. Several wall paintings indeed show bodhisattva playing on the flute, the pipa and other instruments. In this same cave, numerous scenes featuring episodes from the former lives of the Buddha, jataka, *alternate with scenes of prediction (opposite).*

Kashgar, meeting point of the routes of the Takla Makan Desert

The men's clothing consists of a very loose cotton shirt, fastened with a belt and coming down to the calf. It is always worn outside trousers that are very wide and equally made of cotton, and that are secured round the waist with a rope. The trousers are tucked into boots with a broad, square toe and very high heel, the boots themselves being very heavy and clumsy and made of poorly prepared leather which pales very quickly. Well-dressed men do not wear boots but stockings made of supple leather, putting on shoes over these when they go out. Together with stockings of cotton cloth and a little round skullcap, more or less decorated, this is the entire summer costume, as casual dress.

Kashgar, at the point where the northern and southern routes of the Takla Makan Desert meet, was formerly a privileged place of exchange between caravans coming from the West and those from China. Islam is followed by almost three-quarters of the population.

Scented herbs are both used and abused, among them mint, aniseed and coriander, as well as garlic and red pepper. Indian spices, pepper, ginger, zarcheva, cloves, saffron, nutmeg and cinnamon are greatly appreciated, but their dearness prevents them from being consumed in any great quantity and the many curative powers that they are said to have makes them used more frequently as remedies than as culinary extras.

J.-L. DUTREUIL DE RHINS and F. GRENARD, *Scientific Mission to Upper Asia*

The tomb of the scented wife

From what is said, Kashgar was formerly a free kingdom, but at the present time it is ruled by the Great Khan. The people there worship Mahomet ... Many clothes and goods come here. People live on their trades and their trading, and especially on cotton-making. They have very fine gardens and vines and fine orchards of fruit trees. The earth is fertile, and produces all that is necessary in life, for the land is temperate. Cotton here grows together with flax and hemp and many other things. Many merchants set out from this land, and visit many people.

MARCO POLO,
Description of the World

At Kashgar, Islam superseded Buddhism towards the end of the 10th century. The Hodja family, who controlled the region down to the 17th century, claimed to be descended from Mahomet. Aba Hodja had a splended mausoleum built here, covered with green tiles. It is also known as the Tomb of Xiangfei, the 'scented wife', from the name of the concubine of Khozi Khan, the sovereign of Yarkand, who is said to have been captured and taken to Peking at the time of the fall of Kashgar and Yarkand in 1759. According to legend, this pretty Moslem girl, who had been nicknamed because of the perfume that emanated from her everywhere, never succumbed to the advances of the Emperor of China.

On leaving Kashgar for India and the holy places of Buddhism, travellers would pass through lonely spots that were full of danger.

'At the centre of four mountains, which are part of the eastern chain of the Congling Mountains, there is a region which is about a hundred *qing* in area (1000 Chinese acres). In the middle, as down below, one can see, winter and summer, huge heaps of snow, and there are frequent whirlwinds and an icy cold. The fields are seeped in salt, and grain does not grow there. There are no trees at all, and one only sees a few feeble patches of grass. Even during the time of great heat, there is much wind and snow. Scarcely have travellers entered the region than they are in the midst of mists and clouds. Merchants who come and go suffer cruelly in these difficult and dangerous places' (Xuanzang, *Xiyu Ji,* Memoirs of Western Lands, 12).

IN THE STEPS OF THE BUDDHA

THE ROUTES OF INDIA

Via the Kunjerab Pass, you come to what is now Pakistan, in the former kingdoms of Uddiyana and Gandara. After leaving Gilgit and crossing the Indus, you come to Taxila, a little to the west of present Islamabad. The high places of Buddhism that were concentrated in this region contained many traditions relating to the Buddha. In Uddiyana, Buddhism took a Tantric turn, cultivating the practice of mantras and magic formulas. Xuanzang, like Faxian, saw a footprint of the Buddha there, left, it was said, by the buddha Tathagatha after he had tamed a dragon. This footprint appeared long or short depending on the virtue of the person who saw it.

At Gandara, besides numerous stupas, Xuanzang naw a miraculous statue of the Buddha. This statue moved, so that one night, when robbers came, it walked towards them and the thieves fled in fear.

In India, there is no special route that was followed by pilgrims as they made their way through the high places of Buddhism. Even so, the main sites where Buddhism has left its most noticeable traces were located for the most part along the valley of the Ganges, with the special exception of Mathura (Muttra). This latter place preserved several relics in its stupas. Xuanzang records that each year, in the six fastdays of the first, fifth and ninth months, 'everyone flocks to honour the stupas. Banners decorated with pearls are flown and rich parasols are paraded with ceremony. Clouds of scent and a continuous rain of flowers blot out the sun and moon'.

At Sravasti (Sahet-Mahet), the former capital of the kingdom of King Prasenajit, protector of the Buddha Sakyamuni, Xuanzang saw the ruins of the royal palace, as well as numerous stupas commemorating episodes in the life of the Buddha. At Kapilavastu (Tilaura Kot), further to the north (in present Nepal), Xuanzang lingered at the birthplace of Prince Siddharta, who would later be-

Opposite: Several passes enable travellers to cross the Pamirs, such as those of Kunjerab and Minteke between China and Pakistan, and Wakhjir between China and Afghanistan. The yaks that thrive in these parts had greatly impressed Marco Polo because of their long hair.

come the Buddha. On the ruins of the palace of King Suddhodana, his father, a monastery had been built. All the places marking stages in the life of the Buddha were indicated by stupas and venerated. Xuanzang also visited Kusinagara (Kushinagar, not far from Gorakhpur), a ruined town where the Buddha entered nirvana, at the age of eighty. There was a monastery there containing a statue of the Buddha lying, his head turned to the north, at the moment when he entered nirvana. Near Benares (Varanasi), where Buddhism had made very few converts, most of the inhabitants were Hindus, and Xuanzang notices three pools guarded by dragons. The Buddha had bathed here, washing his bowl as well as his monastic habit. A stone marks the spot.

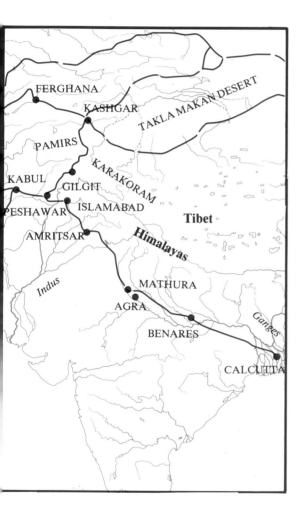

On both sides of the Sino-Pakistani frontier, at Kashgar as well as on the road to Peshawar, the camel is used for transport mainly in the plains, whether as a draught animal or when pack-saddled.

Xuanzang also went to Vaisali (Besarh, to the north of Patna), where the second Buddhist council was held, in which discipline was discussed. But above all else, he stayed at Bodh-Gaya. Nearby, stood the Tree of the Bodhi (the Awakening), under which the Buddha attained enlightenment. This tree, called *pippala,* was several hundred feet high at the time of the Buddha but, says Xuanzang, some wicked kings had cut and lopped it, so that now it was only about fifty feet high. Xuanzang also went to Rajagriha (near Rajgir), former capital of the kingdom of Magadha, where King Bimbisara reigned and where the first Buddhist council was held. He stayed similarly at Nalanda, the site of an important monastery, a virtual Buddhist university famous for its high standard. A little later, the pilgrim Yijing, who had come by sea, studied there for ten years, from AD 675 to 685.

We followed the chain to the south-west, walking for fifteen days. This route is extremely difficult and tiring, and full of obstacles and dangerous drops. All you can see in the mountains are rockfaces, eight thousand feet up. When you approach them your sight becomes blurred. And if, as you walk on, your foot should chance to slip, there is nothing that can hold it.

GAOSENG FAXIAN ZHUAN,
*Foguo Ji, Account of the
Buddhist Kingdoms*

Crossing the Pamirs has always proved to be a difficult venture. The Pamirs form a plateau at the point where the Tianshan, Karakorum and Hindu Kush Mountains meet. Their average altitude is 3000 metres, with some peaks reaching 7000 metres.

Page spread overleaf: At the foot of the Pamirs, on both the Chinese and the Soviet side, the Kirghiz nomads raise yaks, sheep and horses. The Kirghiz were once, in the 9th century, at the head of a vast kingdom that extended as far as Lake Baikal.

137

Tiaoyang, the 'dispute of the sheep'

The Tadzhik Autonomous District has Tashkurgan as its centre, with the town perhaps being the Stone Tower mentioned by Ptolemy. At one time, under the Han, it was probably the city-state of Puli. Xuanzang describes this kingdom under the name of Qiepantuao. The inhabitants seemed rather uncivilised to him: 'Their behaviour is not in the least governed by the principles of ritual. There are few men who cultivated literacy. As they are fierce and violent by nature, they also have impetuous courage.'

A sport greatly appreciated by the Tadzhiks is the 'dispute of the sheep', tiaoyang, *in the course of which horsemen compete to gain possession of a sheep or a decapitated buck. This is the famous* bouzkachi *of Afghanistan.*

Minorities
of the Pamirs

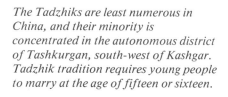

The Tadzhiks are least numerous in China, and their minority is concentrated in the autonomous district of Tashkurgan, south-west of Kashgar. Tadzhik tradition requires young people to marry at the age of fifteen or sixteen.

Page spread overleaf: The Kirghiz are nomadic only in summer. They then live in yurts, which they transport on camelback. In winter, they settle in their crude brick houses at the foot of the mountains.

The passes of
the high Pamirs

In the second moon of winter, Faxian and three others came at midnight to the Little Mountains of Snow. Snow gathers on the mountains in summer and winter alike. From the north, the cold is excessive, and its keenness is such that you almost perish. It was only Huijing who could withstand its severity and who felt it possible to go further. A white froth came out of his mouth. He said to Faxian: 'It is impossible for me to go back. Set off immediately: we must not all die here.' Theeupon, he expired.

GAOSENG FAXIAN ZHUAN,
Foguo Ji, Account of the Buddhist Kingdoms

Once over the Kunjerab Pass between China and Pakistan, the route makes its way to Gilgit. It then rejoins the upper course of the Indus, which rises in the Great Himalayas. Running past the Nangu Parbat massif, it flows into impressive ravines.

Ladak

The evacuation of Sir Aurel Stein to Ladak, after his feet were frost-bitten: 'Then we followed the Karakorum route, marked out by the skeletons of pack animals, sad mementoes of the constant succession of victims who had succumbed to the harsh physical conditions. And on 3rd October we crossed the Karakorum Pass, 18,687 feet above sea level, and with it the frontier between China and India ... I was carried over the glacier slopes and moraines of the Sasser Pass, with the Ladak coolies, patient and good spirited, doing their best to spare me any dangerous falls on ice or snow. But I was sad to think how a few weeks earlier I had rejoiced at the sight of such a grand mountain landscape and of such a climb over a glacier.'

SIR AUREL STEIN, *Ruins of Desert Cathay*

At the frontier between Tibet, India and Pakistan, Ladak remained a stronghold of Buddhism, basically in its Tibetan form.

Half the population lives in the region of Leh. This town was the departure point of several British archaeological expeditions to Central Asia at the end of the 19th century and beginning of the 20th century. From Leh, one could use the Karakorum Pass to reach Kargalik, Yarkand and the route across the south of the Takla Makan Desert.

In the heart
of Gandhara

The edges of the mountains rise up like walls. In one of the stone walls, at the eastern edge, there is a wide, deep cave which is the dwelling-place of the dragon Gopala. The footpath that leads to it is small and narrow; the cave is dark and gloomy. The stones that form the eastern edge sweat continuously, and the water that flows down comes on to the path. Formerly, the ghost of the Buddha could be seen here, as radiant as his natural figure, and offering all

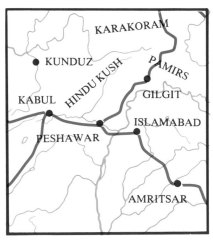

Buddhist images have been found engraved in the rock 130 kilometres south of Gilgit, at Chilas, on the upper course of the Indus. It is believed that they dated from the 5th and 6th centuries.

Peshawar (opposite) is on a road linking Pakistan and Afghanistan via the Khyber Pass, and is at the heart of the former kingdom of Gandhara. The artistic riches of its museum do not detract from the great commercial activity here.

his signs of beauty. It was just like the Buddha when he was alive. Over the past centuries, it has no longer been possible to see it completely. Although you can make out something, it has only a feeble and uncertain likeness. When a man prays with a sincere faith, and has received a secret impression, he sees it clearly. But he cannot enjoy his view for long.

XUANZANG, *Xiyu Ji, Memoirs of Western Lands, 2*

The Taj Mahal

The clothes of the heretics are very varied and differ according to fashion. Some wear a peacock's tail feather, others adorn themselves with strings of skull bones. The latter wear no clothes at all and remain quite naked, while the former cover their bodies with layers of plaited grass. Some tear out their hair and cut their moustaches, while others wear tufted side whiskers and knot their hair on the top of their head.

XUANZANG, *Xiyu Ji, 2*

The Taj Mahal at Agra (page left) is certainly one of the most famous monuments in India. It was built between 1632 and 1643 by Shah Jahan in memory of his wife, the beautiful Mumtaz Mahal, the Chosen One of the Palace.

The Ganges, sacred river of the Hindus

The Ganges fascinated Xuanzang, just as it fascinates still: 'Near its source, this river is three *li* wide. At its mouth, its width is about ten *li*. Its waters are bluish, but often vary in colour, and its waves flow for a great distance. A great number of wonderful creatures live in it, although they are harmless for men. The water has a sweet and pleasant smell and carries with it an extremely fine sand. In Indian texts, it is called "the Water of Happiness". Those who bathe in it, we are led to believe, are purified from all their sins. Those

The Ganges, over 2700 kilometres in length, and the sacred river of the Hindus, is said by them to have waters with purificative and curative properties.

A few kilometres from Benares flowed the Nairanjana river, in which the Buddha bathed before sitting under the Tree of Awakening.

who drink from it, or who simply wash their mouth, find that the ills that threatened them vanish. Those who are drowned in it are reborn among the gods. A mass of men and women are constantly gathered on its banks.'

XUANZANG, *Xiyu Ji, 4*

The Diamond Throne under the Tree of Awakening

The trunk of the Tree is yellowish white, and its leaves, which are green and shining, fall in neither summer nor winter. However, when the anniversary of Nirvana comes, they detach themselves to be reborn the following day in just as much beauty. On that day, the kings and lords meet under its branches, water it with milk, light lamps, spread flowers, and withdraw after picking some of its leaves.

HUILI *and* YANZONG,
Biography of Xuanzang, 3

It was under the Tree of Awakening, at Bodh-Gaya, that the Buddha attained enlightenment. Sitting at the foot of the tree on a seat that had miraculously arisen, the Diamond Throne, the Buddha meditated on suffering and the cycle of rebirths. Resisting the attacks of Mara, the devil, he attained perfect wisdom. In suppressing the thirst of existence, universal suffering was suppressed.

After leaving the Little Pamirs for the west, the route joins the upper course of the Amu Darya. On entering northern Afghanistan, via Feyzabad and Kunduz, one can reach Balkh where the pilgrim Xuanzang also stayed for a while, as did Marco Polo. The latter told of a legend current in the place according to which Alexander the Great was said to have taken the daughter of Darius, king of the Persians, as his wife, precisely there, at Bactres (Balkh). From Balkh, the route can be followed towards Merv or in the direction of Meshel and the south of the Caspian Sea. Further south again is Bamiyan, west of Kabul, which one can also reach from Peshawar. The famous huge statues of the Buddha, which could still be seen not long ago, had already been commented on by Xuanzang. 'To the north-east of the royal town, by the mountainside, there is a stone statue of the Buddha standing. It is from one hundred and forty to one hundred and fifty feet high. Its golden colour is dazzling, and its precious ornaments glow magnificently, To the east (of this statue) there is a monastery which was founded by a former king of this country. To the east of the monastery, there is a statue of the Buddha Sakyamuni standing, made of brass and more than a hundred feet high. The body has been founded in sections, which have then been united to complete and raise (the statue). Two or three *li* to the east of the town, in a monastery, there is a statue of the Buddha lying and entering nirvana, in length over a thousand feet'.

FROM THE PAMIRS TO BAGHDAD

Another pilgrim, Korean this time, Hye-č'o (in Chinese Huichao), also went to Bamiyan at the beginning of the 8th century, as he writes in his account of his journey to India, *Wang Wu Tianzhuguo Zhuan*.

From the region of Bamiyan or from Balkh, the route continues west to Herat. Ghiyath-ed Din used exactly this route from Herat to Balkh, both for the outward and the return journey during his mission to China of 1420–1421. Herat was then the capital of Shah Rokh. At that time, China under the Ming maintained close contact with this kingdom. A little later, in 1432, the emperor Xuanzong of the Ming (*xuande* era) dispatched a eunuch bearing a letter of encouragement on commercial exchanges: 'Let the merchants of our countries travel and trade as they think best'.

Alas, the envoy never arrived at Herat. However, a few years later, another envoy, Chen Cheng (died 1457) reached it. He even left a description of the town and its customs, which were included in his *Shi Xiyu Ji* (Tale of a messenger to the western regions). 'The men shave their heads and are wrapped in a piece of white cloth. The women cover their heads and leave just openings for their eyes. White is regarded as the colour of joy, while black is the colour of mourning. (In China, white is the colour of mourning.) When superiors and inferiors speak to each other, they simply address each other by name. When they meet, they bow slightly and bend the knee three times. For a meal, they use neither spoon nor chopsticks ...'

Opposite: The Khyber Pass, on the frontier between Pakistan and Afghanistan, is the only point of passage between the two countries. Xuanzang passed through it on his way from Lampaka (Lamghan) to Gandhara. Alexander the Great's army also passed through it, as did Genghis Khan much later.

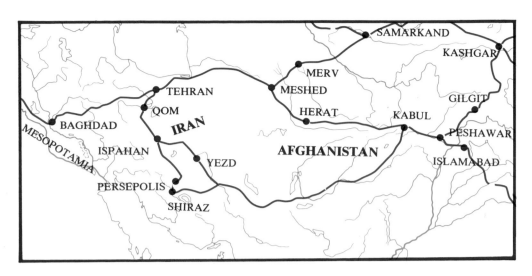

Village of pyramidal type near the Salang Pass north of Kabul, where the land rises to the Hindu Kush. The roofs of the houses serve as terraces for the highest houses.

From Herat, one can pass to the south of the Caspian Sea. This would appear to be the quickest way. But other places now in Iran and Iraq have been traversed by travellers: Kirman, Ispahan, Tabriz, Baghdad or Mosul. At Kirman, Marco Polo especially noted the turquoises which were very abundant. He also observed that in all the big Persian cities 'there are numerous merchants and artisans, who live on trade and labour, for they make golden and silken cloths'.

Tabriz (Marco Polo's Tauris) was a very important place of commercial exchange, with most of the trade involving cloth and clothing. 'The city is so happily situated that other merchants from Baudac (Baghdad), India, Mosul, Curmos (Ormuz) and many other places come here with ease. Also many Latin merchants often come here, especially Genoese, to buy those commodities that come from foreign lands. They also buy precious stones and pearls in great

To the north of the Hindu Kush, the village of Saidabad has houses with dome-shaped roofs. Asian poplar trees are used for building the houses and are planted to mark the occasion of a birth.

quantity. It is thus a city of great trade, and merchants make great profit here'. Tabriz was in effect a junction for several routes from the East at a time before the development of zones controlled by Venetian and Genoese merchants. Baghdad, too, was a great commercial centre. It was the residence of the Abbasid caliph from the 8th century until 1258, when the Abbasids were overthrown by Hulagu, brother of the Great Khan Mangu. Apart from Marco Polo, another traveller who has left us a description of Baghdad is Chang De, who was sent by Mangu in 1259 to serve with his brother. 'The city is divided into a western part and a eastern part. A broad river separates them. The western part had no walls, but the eastern part was fortified. Its walls were built with great bricks. Their upper part formed a splendid edifice ... The caliph's palace was built with scented wood. The walls were built with white and black jade. It is impossible to imagine the quantity of gold and precious stones that was found there ...'

The Cliff of Bamiyan

In the eastern part of the Cliff of Bamiyan (opposite), among hundreds of hollows cut out of the rock, is the fresco-covered recess of the 'Little Buddha', 35 metres high (5th century). To the left are the monastery caves with their sanctuaries, meeting-halls and cells.

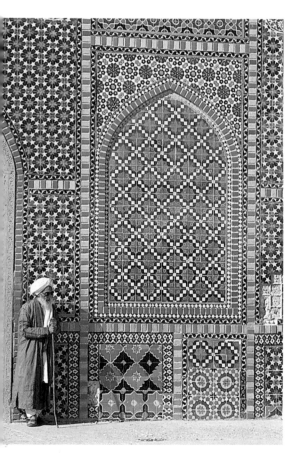

Blind beggar at the Mausoleum of Hazrat Ali at Mazar-e Sharif. This mausoleum was built at the end of the 15th century by the Timurid sultan Hussain Baiqara.

The citadel of Bam

Near Zahedan, in southern Iran, this signal-tower resembles the watch-towers of the Great Wall of China. Brick-built, in the 11th century, it is 15 metres high.

In Persia, which is entirely bare of wood and stone, all the towns (with the exception of a few houses) are built of earth, but of an earth or type of clay so solid that it is cut with ease like turves, having acquired a good consistency. The walls are made by beds or layers in proportion to what is to be hoisted, and between the layers, which are each three feet thick, two or three rows of sun-baked bricks are laid. These bricks are made in a square mould, three finger's breadths high and seven or eight inches wide and, lest they split when drying in the sun, crushed straw is placed on top of them, preventing them from cracking in the great heat. The second layer is not laid until the first is dry, and this second layer must be less wide than the one underneath, so going in proportion. But if care is not taken, these structures sometimes become so narrow as they rise that at the fourth or fifth layer there is not enough thickness to add a further layer. The buildings that are made of these sun-baked bricks are quite clean and, when the wall has been raised, the mason coats it with mortar made of the clay that I mentioned, in such a way that, when all the faults are covered with it, the wall appears quite united.

J. B. TAVERNIER (born 1605),
Six Journeys to Turkey and Persia

Right: The former citadel of Bam was surrounded by a threefold wall. The town dates from the Sassanid empire, but the present ruins only go back to the Safavids. It was destroyed and abandoned in the 18th century.

The ruins of
Ghagha-shahr

The bottom of the slope, to the south, is covered in the remains of halls and vaulted corridors alongside irregular terraces and frequently, it appears, built in tiers. Rubble and rubbish filled the lower halls of which the majority were probably abandoned when the place was still inhabited.

SIR AUREL STEIN,
Innermost Asia

In the middle of Lake Hamoun, on the Hilmand river, not far from Zabol on the Irano-Afhgan frontier, are the ruins of Ghagha-shahr, which were explored by Sir Aurel Stein. Also there is the Parthian town of Kuh-i Kvadja.

From there, you come to Tcheelminar, where I have been several times, among others in the company of Mr Angel, a Dutchman who had been sent by the Company to teach the King of Persia (who was then Cha-Abas II) how to draw. He stayed over a week drawing all these ruins, of which I have seen other drawings showing it to

The great ruins of Persepolis evoke the grand city founded by Darius I at the end of the 6th century BC. This was enlarged by Xerxes and destroyed in 331 BC by Alexander the Great.

be a very fine thing. But after he had finished his own drawing, he declared that he had wasted his time and that the thing was not worth the trouble of drawing, nor to compel a sightseer to turn aside for a quarter of an hour from his journey.

J. B. TAVERNIER,
Six Journeys to Turkey and Persia

The Great Palace (left) was over 100 metres long. It was built on a terrace and the stairway that led to it was decorated with Persian guards.

171

The Palace
of the Persian Kings

For after all they are only old columns, some upright, others lying, and a few badly made figures, with little dark, square rooms. All that together easily persuades those who, like me, have seen the main pagodas of India, which I have examined closely, that Tcheelminar was formerly nothing other than a temple to false gods.

J. B. TAVERNIER,
Six Journeys to Turkey and Persia

Left: The Palace of Xerxes. Opposite: The Palace of a Hundred Columns, built by Artaxerxes I (465 – 424 BC). The gate posts were decorated with sculptures of Persian heroes.

The Kashgai of Fars

The Kashgai, nomadic shepherds of
Fars, number almost 150,000 people
separated into five tribes, each divided
into groups and subgroups. Their origin
has not been clearly established. It is
certain that they have been living in Fars
for about three hundred years, but it is
not known whether they came from the
Caucasus or whether they are the
descendants of the hordes of Genghis
Khan and Tamerlane.
While the men guard the flocks, hunt,
and prepare tea, the women spin wool,
weave carpets and milk the goats. The
establishment of a road system and the
encroachment of crops into the pasture
zones is hastening the end of this
migratory way of life.

The Kashgai, who are Turkish speakers,
lead a semi-nomadic way of life, like
many other, more eastern peoples. In
the summer, they roam north of Shiraz,
returning south to winter with their
goats and sheep. Their community is
organised with families living in groups
of 40 to over 100 tents. These families
themselves constitute clans whose
census cannot be taken with any great
accuracy.

Camels, caravans, caravanserais

Camels are sometimes dressed in festive harness.

In the Iranian east, camel caravans transported goods until a few years ago.

Even if the southern crossing of the Lut desert, between Zahedan and Bam, is now made by motorised transport, camels still have their uses.

Opposite: This ruined caravanserai dates from the 12th century. Travellers stopped here to rest and for refreshment. It was also a place where goods could be traded.

Shi'ites and Zoroastrians

The diversity that exists among Moslems does not consist of the different interpretations that they make of the Koran, but of the different opinions that they hold of the original successors of Mahomet. From these differences have arisen in particular two entirely opposed sects, one known as the sect of the Sunnis, and the other the sect of the Shi'ites ... The sect that the

In north-east Iran, Meshed, a former staging post on the Silk Road, is the holy town of the Shi'ites. Ali Rezam, eighth imam of the Shi'ites, who would succeed Caliph Mamoum at the beginning of the 9th century, was buried here, after eating grapes. The Shi'ites believed that he had been poisoned and made him a martyr.

Persians follow is that of the Shi'ites. They hold in horror the first three successors of Mahomet, Abu-baker, Omar and Osman, and believe that they usurped the succession to Mahomet which should gave gone to Ali, his nephew and son-in-law. They say that this succession consists of eleven pontiffs who descended from Ali and who with him make the number up to twelve.

J. B. TAVERNIER,
Six Journeys to Turkey and Persia

In the region of Yazd, in central Iran, Zorastrianism is still practised, as can be seen in the little village of Mubarak.

Page spread overleaf: Two of the faces of Iran today. Left, a crowd of women wearing traditional dress in the square of Ispahan. Right, a demonstration by young Shi'ites at Meshed.

The carpets of Ispahan

Ispahan has remained famous for its carpet weaving, so that the description 'Ispahan carpet' has long been extended to carpets woven at Herat or Tabriz.

From the corner of this side that faces east to a mosque to the other corner that faces west, this is an area of booksellers and binders and cabinet-makers. In the middle of the southern side there is a great gateway with a tower each side. This leads to a

mosque whose gate is covered in silver leaf, and it is assuredly the most beautiful gate and the most beautiful entrance of all the mosques in Persia.

J. B. TAVERNIER,
Six Journeys to Turkey and Persia

Ispahan still has several mosques of the Seljukian and Safavid dynasties. On the square of Maidan-i-Shah, the Masjid-i-Shah was built between 1611 and 1629 by Shah Abbas I.

The route that passes north of the Tien Shan chain, where it forms the third overland approach to China from the west, is hardly mentioned by Chinese writers before the 3rd century, and even then, somewhat vaguely. It seems that several passes probably linked this route with the one south of the Tien Shan Mountains, either between Lake Barköl and Hami, or between Turfan and Jimusa (formerly Beshbalik, the Uigur capital, known to the Chinese as Beiting). To the west, the route runs through the Ili valley.

From Kucha, through the Bedel Pass, you come to Lake Issyk-Kul. This was the route followed by Xuanzang on his outward journey. Near Suye (Tokmak), Xuanzang met the Turkish khan, and he was struck by the royal residence and ostentatious display. 'The khan lived in a great tent which was decorated with golden flowers, whose brilliance dazzled the eyes. The official ushers had spread long mats at the entrance, and they sat on these in two rows. They were all wearing bright costumes of silk brocade. The khan's personal guard stood behind them. Although he was a barbarian prince, living in a felt tent, you couldn't help looking at him without experiencing a feeling of admiration and respect' (Huili and Yanzong, *Biography of Xuanzang,* 2).

THE
ROAD TO SAMARKAND

It was in this region that the Wusun had formerly settled, and where Zhang Qian had passed. The kingdoms crossed by Xuanzang, and where now the towns of Frunze or Tashkent stand, did not noticeably attract his attention, with the exception of the Land of a Thousand Springs, whose softness contrasted sharply with the harshness of the countries through which he had just travelled. 'The land is abundantly watered, and the trees of the forests offer the finest vegetation. In the latter spring months, the most varied flowers shine on the ground, like a rich embroidery. There are a thousand streams of running water, and this gives the name of a Thousand Springs. The khan of the Turks comes here each year to avoid the summer heat. You can see a whole number of stags, decorated with little bells and rings. They are used to human beings, and do not flee when they see them. The khan is fond of them and enjoys seeing them. He has addressed a decree to his subjects in which he says that whoever kills one of them will be punished by death, without remission. That is why all the stags can peacefully end their days here' (*Xiyu Ji,* 1).

Although Xuanzang said nothing about it, these regions have had an active Buddhist past, as proved by several archaeological finds. At Ak-Beshim, for example, in the Zhu valley, near Frunze, two Buddhist temples have been discovered, dating probably from the 7th or 8th century. Similarly, traces of Buddhist worship have been found at Saryg and Dzhul, near Frunze, and also at Kuva, further south, in the eastern Ferghana Valley. Mention should also be made of the Buddhist monastery of Adjina-Tepe in Tadzhikistan, a little to the north of the Amu Darya. This is an important site where wall paintings and sculptures have been found. Not far from Samarkand is Pendzhikent, the an-

Opposite: Girl of the Kazakh minority living at the foot of the Celestial Mountains, Tien Shan, in the north of the country.

Along the upper course of the Ili, in the Nilk pastureland, the Kazakhs raise several hundred thousand horses. From the time of the Han dynasty, the horses raised by the Wusun here were of particularly fine quality.

Opposite: The Kazakhs who live in the north of the Tien Shan Mountains still preserve a nomadic way of life, but only in summer. They then live in yurts, bao in Chinese). In winter, they come down to live in houses at the foot of the mountains.

cient capital of a Sogdian principality, and at its height in the 7th and beginning of the 8th centuries. It is famous for its wall paintings which decorate the houses of noblemen and merchants. The ninety manuscripts discovered on Mount Mugh, mostly in Sogdian, have shed a new light on the history of Sogdiana and on the economic life of Sogdian society.

As for Afrasiab, situated in the old part of Samarkand, and believed to have been the town of Marakanda described by the Roman historian Quintus Curtius Rufus, it was an important trading centre. Xuanzang stayed there and became interested in this part of the country as much for its natural wealth as for its commercial activity. 'The kingdom of Samojian (Samarkand) has a circumference of sixteen to seventeen hundred *li*. It is elongated from east to west, and constricted from north to south. It is protected by natural obstacles and has a large population. The most valuable products of foreign countries are amassed in great number in this kingdom. The soil is thick and fertile and gives abundant harvests. The trees of the forests offer a magnificent vegetation, and flowers and fruit are abundant. This land provides a great number of excellent horses. The inhabitants are distinguished from those of other lands by their great skill in arts and crafts' (*Xiyu Ji*).

The Sogdians were especially noted in China for their commercial activity. One Wei Jie observes this in a 'Memoir on the Barbarians of the West', quoted in an encyclopaedia of the late 8th century, the *Tongdian,* written by Du You. 'They are all clever traders. When a boy reaches the age of five years, he is sent to study books. When he begins to understand them, he is sent to study trade. To make profits is regarded by most of the inhabitants as an excellent thing'.

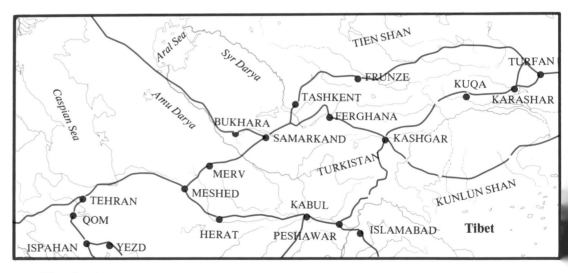

The further one goes westwards, the more the different routes multiply. From Tashkent, along the Syr Darya (the former Iaxartes) and the Aral Sea, one came to the Caspian Sea. This was the route followed by Joannes de Plano Carpini. It was also possible to follow the course of the Amu Darya (the Oxus) to reach the Aral Sea and the Caspian. This was very likely the route taken by Matteo and Niccolò Polo. Finally, one could proceed directly south-west in the direction of Merv and to the south of the Caspian Sea, and join up with the more southerly routes. Once the Caspian Sea had been rounded, rather than crossed, travellers following a northern route came to the Sea of Azov or headed for the Caucasus and Turkey.

The nomads of the Ili valley

Right: The plain of the Ili river, north of the Tien Shan Mountains, was at one time disputed territory between the Xiongnu and the Wusun. The problems concerning the frontier between China and Russia in the 19th century were regulated by the Ili treaty of 1880. Opposite, the frontier post of Qungshui.

The Mongol-style yurt, used by nomadic shepherds from Mongolia to Central Asia, is about 5 metres in diameter and 3 metres high. The walls are of felt stretched on a wooden framework. The ground is usually covered with carpets.

Preceding page spread: The Celestial Mountains, Tien Shan, extend for 2000 kilometres from east to west and 400 kilometres from north to south. They rise to a height of 5000 metres, and form a barrier between the Takla Makan Desert and the Dzungarian plain.

They build the houses where they sleep on a circular base of woven rods. The framework of the house is made of rods which converge towards the top in a circular opening from which there leads a sort of duct similar to a chimney. They cover the framework with white felt which they coat fairly frequently with lime or white earth and powdered bone so as to heighten the brightness of the white.

The Kazakhs live either side of the Sino-Soviet border. In the USSR, they occupy a federal republic that extends to the Caspian Sea, but in it they are no more than a minority, forming a little over 40% of the population. This is because of the large numbers of immigrant Russians and Ukrainians.

In the diversity of its faces, the population of Central Asia reflects the multiplicity of travellers who once followed the Silk Road.

Sometimes, too, they use black felt.

They have no fixed dwelling and never know where they will be the following day ... Each captain, depending whether he has more or fewer men under him, knows the limits of his pastureland, and he knows where he must graze his animals in winter and summer, spring and autumn.

WILLIAM OF RUYSBROECK,
Journey to the Mongol Empire

The Kazakhs raise camels, too. Today there are still around 200,000 of them in the republic of Kazakhstan.

The Arab conquest of Central Asia in the 7th century was much slower than that of the Sassanid empire, but Islam is still widely found there.

191

Tashkent

Both men and women plait their hair. The men's bonnets look like hills when seen in the distance. They are embroidered and decorated with pompoms. All the officials wear such bonnets. People of lower rank cover their head with a piece of white muslin about six feet long. The wives of the chiefs and the richest men wrap their head in a piece of gauze five or six feet long and black or dark red in colour. Flowers and plants are ambroidered everywhere.

LI JICHANG
Xiyu Ji,
Account of a Journey to the West

Tashkent, formerly known under the name of Shash, does not have a past as rich as that of Samarkand or Bukhara. In the 11th century, Al-Biruni identified it as the Stone Town mentioned by Ptolemy. It still played an important role in the time of Tamerlane.

Opposite: The mosque of the khodja Ahmed Yasebi dates from the 16th century. Ahmed (died 1503), who was one of the sons of Yunuz, Khan of the Djaghataides, reigned over the region of Ili and Turfan while his brother Mahmoud was in power at Tashkent.

The carpet market

Although it is a barbarian town (Maracanda, Samarkand), you find carpets dyed in a matchless purple shade, if not that of wine sparkling in a cup in the sun, and so thick that in treading on them it is like sailing on a galley ship.

CATULLUS, *born 87* BC

The king (Shah Abbas II) entered by a door that led from his apartment into the hall, followed only by thirteen eunuchs to guard him and two venerable old men, whose office is to take off the king's shoes when he enters the chambers with their gold and silk carpets and to put them on again when he goes out.

J. B. TAVERNIER,
Six Journeys to Turkey and Persia

The bazaar at Tashkent is held on Sundays. One of the principal activities is the selling of woollen carpets.

Ferghana and its 'celestial horses'

Opposite: The Ferghana Valley has always been noted for its fine horses. It was here that the 'celestial horses' so coveted by Emperor Wu of the Han were bred.

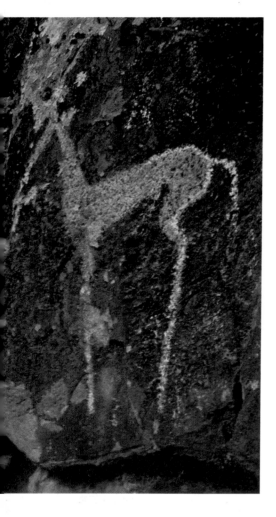

In the region of Osh and Saimaly-Tash, horses are carved in the rock. The date of these pictures is highly conjectural, but the oldest of them could date back to the Bronze Age.

The kingdom of Feihan (Ferghana) is four thousand *li* in circumference. On all sides it is surrounded by mountains. The land is rich and fertile. It produces abundant harvests, and a great quantity of flowers and fruit. The land is fitting for the rearing of sheep and goats. The climate is windy and cold. The men have a firm and brave nature. Their language differs from that of other people, their faces are ugly and crude. For very many years now, this land has had no overall leader. The most powerful men fight among one another with weapons, and remain independent of one another. Felling themselves protected by rivers and natural obstacles, they have marked the limits of their territory, and each one occupies a separate dwelling.

XUANZANG, *Xiyu Ji, 1*

The Pamirs

We travelled on horseback
twelve days over this plain, and
it is called Pamir. During these
twelve days, we saw neither
dwelling nor inn, for it is a
desert the whole length of the
route, and we found nothing to
eat there. Travellers who are
obliged to pass this way find it
best to take provisions with
them. There are no birds to be
found, because of the height and
the intense cold, and because
they would not be able fo find
anything to eat. Moreover, I tell
you that because of the great
cold, fire is not as bright and
burning, nor the same colour as
in other places, and food cannot
be cooked well.

MARCO POLO,
Description of the World

*Tadzhikistan, which extends to the
south of the Ferghana Valley and to the
west of the Pamirs, has a population of
Iranian origin. The Tadzhiks are found
in the USSR, Afghanistan and China.*

198

Zoroastrianism in Kirghizia

Three types of Sogdian ossuaries: in casket form with decorative mouldings (below); so-called 'yurt style', with decorative carving (far below); 'yurt style' with anthropomorphous cover (opposite).

The many funerary relics found in Sogdiana, Chorasmia or Margiana clearly emphasise the influence of Zoroastrianism in Central Asia. The funerary directions of Zoroastrianism involved the corpses exposed to the ravages of birds and dogs. In Central Asia, from the 3rd and 4th centuries, the remains that were found were often preserved in ossuaries, vessels of different shapes.

'... Where shall we bear the bones of the

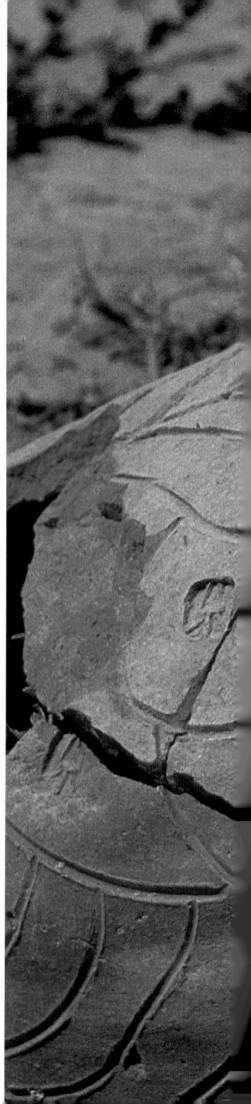

dead, O Ahura Mazdah? Where shall we lay them?

For this purpose an *uzdana* will be made, beyond the reach of dog, fox and wolf, which cannot be made wet from above by the rain waters. If the worshippers of Mazdah have the means, (they will make them) in stone, or in plaster, or in earth ...'

Vendidad, VI, 49 – 51

The mosaics of Samarkand

The city of Samarkand is also very rich in merchandise which comes from all parts. Russia and Turkey send linen and hides. China sends silks, which are the best in the world, and musk, which is not found anywhere else in the world, also rubies and diamonds, pearls, rhubarb and many other things. The merchandise that comes from China is the best and most valuable that arrives in this city, and it could be said that the Chinese are the most skillful craftsmen in the world. They themselves say that they have two eyes, whereas the French have only one and the Moors are blind, so that they are superior to all other countries. From India come spices such as nutmeg, clove, mace, cinnamon, ginger and many others that do not reach Alexandria.

Account of envoy
Ruy Gonzales de Clavijo
at the court of Tamerlane, 1403 – 1406

The central square of Samarkand is called Registan. Ulug Beg (1393 – 1449), son of Shah Rokh, had several mosques built there. The madrasa *Tillia Kari (the Gilded) was built there in the 17th century. Earlier, the* madrasa *Shir Dorr (of the Tigers) had been built.*

Page spread overleaf: Three madrasas, *or theological colleges, are situated around three sides of Registan Square. Apart from the two already mentioned, the* madrasa *of Ulug Beg, which dates from the 15th century, stands opposite the* madrasa *Shir Dorr. All three are covered in Turkish ceramics.*

Merv, ancient capital of Margiana

In southern Turkmenistan, the former town of Gyaur-Kala (Merv), 30 kilometres from present Mary, has been excavated since the end of the 19th century. Its ruins cover a circumference of about 7 kilometres. Situated on the course of the Murgav river before its waters disappear in the Karakorum Desert, it was the capital of Margiana, Alexandria. The huge Erk-Kala fortress was originally built about the 2nd

century BC, and was rebuilt after the Battle of Carrhae (53 BC). The town was conquered by the Arabs in AD 651. The surrounding walls, of which the largest is 15 metres high, and whose ruins are shown here, were built in the 6th century.

Page spread overleaf: The history of Bukhara has generally been linked with that of Samarkand. Bukhara was part of the empire of Tamerlane, becoming first the capital of the Shaybanids (1500–1599), then of the Astrakhanids (1599–1785), and finally of the Mangits until the 19th century. The remains of the walls of this important caravan city date only from the 17th century.

206

The oasis was famous for its fine cotton which it exported either in raw form or as cloth. It was equally famous for the place it occupied in sericulture, with the exporting of raw silk as much as finished silks. The weavers' district, like that of the brassware dealers and that of the potters, was visited by caravans

from the whole of the Middle East. One of the wonders of the city was the mausoleum of Sandjar, whose great dome, turquoise blue in colour, could be seen at a distance of a day's journey.

RENÉ GROUSSET,
The Conqueror of the World

Right: The mausoleum of Sultan Sandjar, who reigned over Khorassan. He was buried there in 1157.

THE ROUTES TO EUROPE

From the routes that meet in Mesopotamia, Kurdistan or Armenia, several routes can still be followed to the final destination of Italy and Western Europe.

First, one can follow the ancient trade routes, with Dura-Europos, Palmyra or Antioch as points of passage, or via Acre at the time of the Crusades. After that, one crosses the Mediterranean Sea. It is still possible to reach Constantinople, either from the Crimea, coming from the north of the Caspian Sea, or from Eastern Turkey, via Trebizond (Trabzon), crossing the Black Sea, and so reaching Italy, again by the sea route.

Dura-Europos, on the banks of the Euphrates, was not only an active trading centre but a military place. Founded as a Macedonian colony in the 3rd century BC, it fell into the hands of the Parthians at the beginning of the 1st century BC and became a fortified town protecting the Euphrates route. As an important caravan town in Partho-Roman trade, it was conquered in AD 165 by the Romans, and lost its activity thereafter.

Palmyra, another caravan town, halfway between the Euphrates and the Mediterranean, was originally known under the name of Tadmor in the 2nd millennium BC. The literary traces that it has left, in addition to important art relics, are better known to us, first from the writings of the Greek historian Appianus, in his *Roman History* (1st century BC), but also from those of Pliny: 'Palmyra, a town famous for its situation, for the richness of its soil and its pleasant waters, has a territory that is surrounded by a vast belt of sands. Separated, so to say, from the rest of the world by nature, it enjoys independence between two powerful empires, the Romans and the Parthians, attracting, in case of disagreement, the prime interest of the one and the other' (*Natural History*).

Flavius Josephus (AD 37 – c. 100) adds that 'it is the only place where those who cross the desert can find fountains and wells' (*Antiquities of the Jews*).

It is a fact that until Palmyra was sacked in AD 272 by Aurelian, the town remained an essential staging post on the Silk Road. The Chinese silks of the Han period that have been discovered here testify to this. Even the importance of the ruins made a strong impression on the Flemish traveller Corneille Lebrun in the 17th century. 'We noticed hundreds of ruins, of such a size that, if one can compare the original beauty that the place formerly had with that which remains now, I doubt whether there by any town in the world that could rival the beauty of this one' (*Journey to the Levant*).

Antioch (now Antakya), with its two ports on the right and left banks of the Orontes, occupied a leading position in Mediterranean trade, rivalling that of Alexandria, at least until the 6th century, when earth tremors and its capture by Khosroes I put paid to its activity.

Not far from Antioch, Laias (sometimes written L'Ayas), in the Gulf of Alexandretta, played a significant role in the trade between Italy and the Middle

Opposite: The routes across Syria, which followed the Tigris or the Euphrates and which crossed Iraq coming from the region of Basra, were used as much by overland travellers coming from southern Iran via Fars and the Zagros Mountains as by those who came from India by sea up the Persian Gulf.

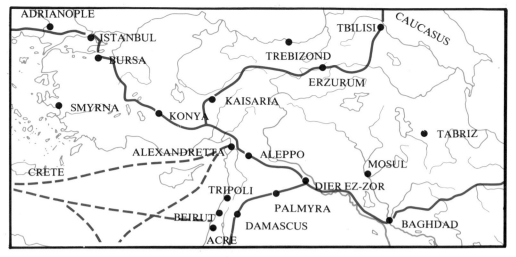

It is called Shiai Catai (tea of China) and grows in the district of Cathay called Cacianfu (Xian). It is freely used and is highly regarded throughout the land. You take some of this herb, whether dry or fresh, and you boil it in water. One or two cups of this brew absorbed into an empty stomach will banish fever, head and stomach aches, pains in the side and joints. It must be taken as hot as you can drink it ... And (this tea) is so highly appreciated and esteemed that all those who set off on a journey take some with them ...

Remarks on China of
HAJJI MOHAMED *made to*
Giovanni Battista Ramusio

East some time later, in the 13th century. William of Ruysbroeck set sail for Cyprus from there on his return journey. Marco Polo spoke of the town thus: 'There is by the sea in the said province a town called Laias, fair and large, and active in trade. For you should know that all the spices and cloths of the Euphrates are brought to this town, and all other precious things. There is cotton in abundance. And the merchants of Venice, Pisa and Genoa, as well as those of all inland regions, come here to buy and sell, and keep their stores here'.

On the Black Sea, Trebizond (Trabzon) also experienced a great commercial boom. A former Greek colony, its prosperity had been long established, as a re-

sult of the land route which came from Tabriz. Between Tabriz and Trebizond, indeed, Marco Polo described Mount Ararat, also called Noah's Mount, for Noah's Ark had run aground there, and it was still visible, it was said, in the time of Marco Polo.

Farther north, in the Crimea, was Soldaia (or Soudak), an important Venetian storehouse centre. Silks and spices of east Asian origin were exported from there, as well as furs and corn from Russia, salted fish from the Sea of Azov, and slaves.

Although tea became the favoured drink of the Middle East, it was long an imported product. The tea-plant has been grown in Iran, Georgia and Turkey for only a few dozen years now.

Hatra, fortress of the Parthians

To the south of Mosul, Hatra was a fortress built by the Parthians to provide a defence against the Roman army in the 1st and 2nd centuries AD.

There is little known of the Parthian civilisation (3rd century BC – 2nd century AD). Written documents are lacking, and only a few monuments provide any evidence of it. One can however see, as at Hatra (Al Hadr) or Kuh-i Khvadja, a particularly marked influence of Greek art.

The palace at Hatra was built in freestone, in the Roman manner. It is perhaps one of the buildings to be most influenced by the Graeco-Roman style.

Opposite: The camels sculpted on the walls of the palace at Hatra invoke the many caravans that visited the city.

The palace at Hatra was built on the plan of an *iwan* house, that is, with vaulted rooms enclosed on three sides but having the fourth open to the outside. At Hatra, two *iwans* stand adjacent to each other with their annexes. Behind the palace is the temple.

The Euphrates, historic arterial route

Hydraulic chain-pumps, or norias, *which are used to raise water to irrigate the crops, are found throughout Asia, from China to the Near East. Mesopotamia is no exception.*

The Euphrates, Al-Furat, rises in Turkey, then crosses Syria and Iraq before joining the Tigris to form the Shatt-al-Arab. Although no important town has been settled on its banks, it has, like the Tigris, served as an arterial route between the Persian Gulf and Anatolia or the Mediterranean.

In the Shatt-al-Arab, the Euphrates flows through marshland. Dwellings here consist of houses made of reeds.

217

The ziggurat, Mesopotamian house of the gods

The mosque in Samarra, situated about 100 km north of Baghdad, is famous for its spiral minaret. Samarra was the ancient capital of caliph Al'Moutasims (9th century).

Thirty kilometres north-west of Baghdad are the ruins of the great ziggurat of Adar Kuf (14th – 15th centuries BC), 57 metres high (right). These gigantic towers of the Mesopotamian culture had a square base and rose with stepped terraces. At the top, a temple or holy cell was the 'terrestial house' of the god, to correspond with his celestial house. The best preserved ziggurat is the one at the city of Ur.

Dura-Europos, at the crossroads of the great religions

Originally a Macedonian colony, founded by Seleucus Nicator in about 280 BC on the right bank of the Euphrates, Dura-Europos fell to the Parthians at the beginning of the 1st century AD. It was then conquered by the Romans in AD 165. After being destroyed in AD 256 by the Sassanid king Shapur I, it was finally abandoned.

Like Palmyra, another caravan centre, it was influenced by Hellenistic art, although less markedly. Paintings revealed by excavations are often the work of itinerant painters, whether Palmyrene, Jewish or Iranian.

The excavations carried out at Dura-Europos since 1932 have revealed a number of temples dedicated to Zeus, Adonis, and others, as well as a Christian baptistry and a synagogue. Its walls, protected by the sands, have come to display a quite exceptional collection of paintings, dating partly from the beginning of the 3rd century and partly from the middle of this same century.

The Bedouins of Syria

At all times, the caravan travels more by night than by day ... For if one arrived at nightfall, it would be difficult in the darkness to arrange all the things, to pitch the tents, rub down the horses, prepare a meal and provide for everything that is necessary for an encampment ...

The camels which go to Persia through the northern provinces of Turkey walk only in

Carpets, which are important for the comfort of Syrian Bedouins, are not knitted but woven on rudimentary looms.

single file and in groups of seven. They are attached to one another by a rope the thickness of the little finger and a span in length. This is fastened to the rear of the load of the camel in front, and is tied at the other end with a little cord made of a sort of wool which passes through a loop hanging from the nostrils of the camel behind.

J. B. TAVERNIER,
Six Journeys to Turkey and Persia

Bedouins have preserved a way of life allied to that of nomadic peoples. They live in tents made of cloth or, sometimes, hide, and their diet consists chiefly of dairy products and meat.

Tobacco is smoked by means of a narghile or hookah, the smoke passing through a long tube linked to a reservoir of perfumed water, where it is cooled and scented before reaching the mouth of the smoker.

223

The life of the nomad stock-breeders

Bedouins raise camels rather than goats, sheep or horses. It is the men who keep watch over the herds while the women do the milking and make the dairy products.

The herds of camels raised by each encampment can amount to several hundred in number. This one (page right) has 212.

The camel, although he is big and works hard, eats very little and contents himself with what he finds in among the heathland, where he specially searches out the thistle, which he likes very much. As soon as the caravan arrives at the place where it is to pitch camp, all the camels belonging to a single master come and take up their positions in a circle and lie down on their four feet, so that when a rope holding the packs in untied, these slip and fall gently to the

ground on either side of the camel. When it is time to load up again, the same camel comes and lies down once more between the packs and, once they are fastened, slowly stands up with his load, which is done in very little time without any difficulty or noise.

J. B. TAVERNIER,
Six Journeys to Turkey and Persia

The forest of columns at Palmyra

We had scarcely passed these ancient monuments than, the mountains dividing on either side, we discovered all at once the greatest quantity of ruins, all of white marble, that we had ever seen ... It is almost impossible to imagine anything more astonishing than this sight. Such a great number of Corinthian pillars with so few solid walls and buildings give the most romantic effect that one could wish to see.

ROBERT WOOD, *The Ruins of Palmyra, visit made in 1751*

It must be acknowledged that antiquity has left nothing, either in Greece or Italy, that is comparable to the magnificence of the ruins of Palmyra.

VOLNEY, *Journey to Egypt and Syria,* 1787

Once a frontier town, Palmyra has revealed the richness of its monuments thanks to the numerous excavations which have been made here. Left, the Great Colonnade, 110 metres in length. Opposite, the triple arch. The columns of the Great Colonnade which line the main street partly hid the buildings which were behind them (page spread overleaf).

The love of horses
and equestrian sports in Asia Minor

They are very skilful with the assegai, and it is a great pleasure to see them in a great open place or in the country with many on horseback. One man begins to run, and another chases after him, following at full speed with an assegai in his hand. This assegai is normally a square stick made of a palm branch, three feet in length and two or three inches thick. When the pursuer is quite close, and almost the length of his stick away, he hurls the assegai at the rider's back – adroitly, with a twist of his hand which doubles its force – so that he receives a strong blow, which sometimes inflicts very considerable wounds, sometimes even on the head. I saw one man in Cairo who had to have a bone taken from his head, after being wounded with an assegai. Now the one who is in front and is being pursued looks sideways while fleeing, as much to lower his head, if this is needed, in an attempt to catch the assegai, and even to break the force of the blow if he can. And so he holds his hand ready behind, and when he catches the assegai, which happens quite often, he runs after the other rider, and both immediately change roles.

JEAN THÉVENOT, *Journey to the Levant,* 1665

In the less arid regions of Turkey, the horse comes into his own. Equestrian sports are especially common.

230

Traditional crafts related to the upkeep of horses and their equipment are still actively pursued. Here, a saddler works in his tiny workshop.

231

However, this book has acquired such a reputation among all these peoples, that they say it was written in heaven, and sent from God to Mahomet by the angel Gabriel during the month of Ramadan, not all at once, but chapter by chapter: and they revere it so greatly, that they never touch it, without carrying it immediately on their heads before reading it. And if someone were to sit on an Alcoran, he would commit a great crime.

In Turkey, the women are normally beautiful, well made and without blemish. They are very pale, for they rarely go out and they are still veiled when they do. They add artifice to their natural beauty, for they paint their eyebrows and eyelids with a blackish colour called surme, which is used by them to lend charm.

JEAN THÉVENOT, *Journey to the Levant*

The wedding, according to tradition, lasts two days and follows a well-ordered procedure.

Opposite: Konya is famous for its ancient monastery of whirling dervishes, mevlevi, *and for the tomb of its founder. Here, an old man reads the Koran.*

The 'fairy chimneys' of Cappadocia

In Cappadocia, man has exploited the extraordinary natural relief, with its peaks and walls of lava, the result of erosion taking place at different rates. He has dug out churches and monasteries by sculpting pillars, columns, vaults and even items of furniture from the walls, such as altars, benches, tables, etc. These monasteries, which superseded the hermitages developed by Basil of Caesarea (Kayseri) in the 4th century, were originally a place of refuge for Christians persecuted by the Romans and the Greeks. The wall paintings that decorated them were destroyed or mutilated by the Arabs in the oldest churches.

The 'fairy chimneys' which have resulted from erosion, and the churches hollowed out of the soft rock, give the valley of Cappadocia a fantastic appearance. Persecuted Christians took refuge here in a network of veritable subterranean cities.

A cocoon market

Bursa (Brussa), in Turkey, is a silk
town. At the time of the annual fair, the
cocoon market attracts a large crowd.

To unwind the silk thread, the cocoons
are plunged into boiling water in order
to dissolve the sericin that binds the
thread.

TO ROME, THE MYSTERIOUS CITY

The last great staging post before Italy, Constantinople (Byzantium) had astounded the Crusaders by its magnificence, and none more than Geoffroi de Villehardouin, at the end of the 11th century. The superb palaces and lofty churches, the length and breadth of the city, gave one to believe that there was no other such powerful city in the world: 'and know that there was no man so bold that his flesh did not quiver' (*The Conquest of Constantinople*).

Villehardouin was not the only one to be amazed at the importance of Constantinople. Most of the great travellers saw it as one of the most outstanding cities in the world, among them Ibn Battuta, in the 14th century. 'It is extremely large and divided into two parts which are separated by a great river, where the ebb and flow can be seen in the same way that it occurs in the river of Sale, a town of Maghreb. There was formerly on this river a stone bridge; but it has been destroyed, and now one crosses the water in boats. The name of the river is Absomy (sic). One of the two parts of the city is called Esthamboul. This is the part that stands on the eastern side of the river, and it is there that the sultan lives, with the great people of his empire and the remainder of the Greek population. Its markets and streets are broad and paved with flagstones. People of each profession occupy a distinct place, which they do not share with those of any other trade. Each market is provided with gates which are closed at night. Most of the craftworkers and merchants there are women' (*Journeys*).

Later, Jean Thévenot (1633 – 1667) would give a concise description of Constantinople, telling among other things of his role as a merchant and more especially of his *hans* or caravanserais. 'These hans are very well built, and the main walls are of freestone. The finest one at Constantinople is called Valida Hhane, Han of the Sultana Mother, because the mother of the Great Lord now reigning

Opposite: Istanbul, because of its situation on the edge of the Bosphorus, separating Europe and Asia, has always occupied an advantageous position on the silk routes, whether by land or sea. The splendour of former Byzantium dates mainly from the reign of Constantine and from the establishment of the Eastern Roman Empire.

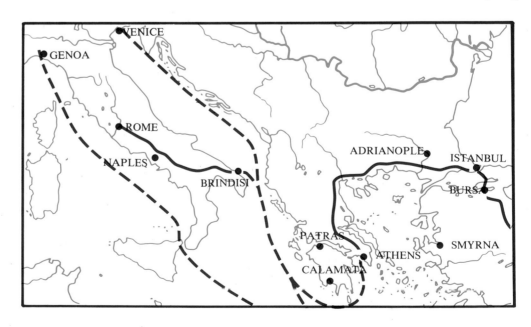

had it built. It is very convenient for foreigners, who can always find a cheap house to rent, having a mattress, some blankets, carpets and cushions, and there you are both furnished and lodged. These hans bring great revenue to those to whom they belong' (*Journey to the Levant*).

Constantinople and Rome have long been more or less confused by Chinese historians, so that the Western Roman Empire, then the Eastern, were successively known as Da Qin, then Fulin. The descriptions of them made in Chinese historic sources were to a greater extent founded on facts featuring in the History of the Han (*Hanshu*), compiled in the 1st century AD, facts which were repeated in successive dynastic histories without any substantial modification. The

The Bosphorus, whose name means 'passage of the bull' or 'bearer of the bull', divides Istanbul into two halves. According to legend, Io, the daughter of the king of Argos, crossed it in the form of a heifer in order to escape the anger of Zeus. It was at its narrowest point, between the fortress of Rumelia and that of Anatolia, that Darius is said to have crossed in 500 BC with more than 700,000 men on a floating bridge.

Roman Empire would long remain a mysterious land in Chinese history and was regarded at the time of the Han as in some measure another China.

The resemblance between the two countries was sometimes overstated. In a Taoist text probably written in the 7th century, the Book of Cinnabar Divine Liquid of Gold of Great Purity (*Taiqing Jinyi Shendan Jing*), chapter 3, the myth is maintained, developed and practically turned upside down by the journey to Da Qin of a Chinese merchant disguised as an envoy who had come to offer silk. 'The ambassador had offered the king a thousand rolls of silk brocade taken from those that he had on the boat. The king said to him laughing: "Those are barbarian silks! What bad quality! When things are of bad quality, it means that the people who have made them are bad! Sincerity is not perfect: they are not things which our country could put to any use!" And he tore them and did not take them. Then he showed the ambassador gauzes with thread as brilliant as jade, silk brocades with flowers in eight colours, blue turquoise satins, silken fabrics woven with jade thread, embroideries of blue stones set with gold. The white was like snow, the red like the flames of the setting sun, the blue was finer than the feathers of kingfishers, the black was like a fluttering raven.

These cloths were of a very bright sheen, the five colours had spread everywhere; these materials were four feet wide; they had no blemish, and as soon as one saw them next to the much blemished cloths of the ambassador, the

silks of the northern land looked truly ridiculous. The ambassador himself said: "In the land of Da Qin, they lack nothing, and all is better than in China! There can never be any comparison! Even in the kitchen stoves, they burn only olibanum. Perfumes are very plentiful. In this country, there is nothing dirty. It is truly a Land of Cockaigne!" That is approximately what the ambassador told on his return. Since that time, no one has dared to return to Da Qin. The merchants have repeated what he had said and have altogether ceased to go to that country'.

The Church of St. Sophia dates from AD 347, in the reign of Constantine. It was subjected to destruction and fire several times, and each time was rebuilt, notably by Emperor Justinian (AD 527–565), who turned it into a sumptuous edifice.

241

St. Sophia

All those who have seen Constantinople are agreed that this city is in the finest situation that there is in the world, so that it seems as if nature has made it to dominate and command the whole earth. A quantity of fine mosques can be seen here, of which the most magnificent is that of St. Sophia, formerly a Christian church, built by the emperor Justin, and enlarged, enriched and decorated by the emperor Justinian, who dedicated it to the wisdom of God. That is why it is named Hagia Sophia.

JEAN THÉVENOT, *Journey to the Levant*

After the fall of Constantinople in 1453, most of the churches were turned into mosques. This was the case with St. Sophia. Since then, it has lost much of its mosaic décor, with the exception of a few fragments.

On the Asian border

The interior of the Grand Bazaar at Istanbul. In the foreground, a silverer's shop with a number of vessels in chased metal.

Carpets and tapestries of fine wool have been sought after in Istanbul at all times. Below, an itinerant merchant.

We walked through the splendid bazaars which form the centre of Stamboul. It was a pure labyrinth built solidly in stone in the Byzantine style and a vast place of shelter from the heat of the day. Huge galleries, some arched, others with ribbed vaulting, with sculpted pillars and colonnades, are each devoted to a particular kind of wares. Above all we admired the clothing and Turkish slippers of the women, the worked and embroidered fabrics, the cashmere, the carpets, the furniture inlaid with gold, silver and mother of pearl, the jewellery, and especially the shining weaponry gathered in that part of the bazaar that is called the bezesteen.

GÉRARD DE NERVAL, *Journey to the East*

Midway between industrialised Europe and the Third World, Turkey has seen new products emerging among its traditional ways of life. Here, Coca Cola and hookahs rub shoulders.

Turkey is an important producer of tobacco, grown in the regions bordering the Aegean Sea, the Mediterranean, and the Sea of Marmara. Older smokers still prefer the hookah.

245

The Grand Bazaar

Istanbul has always been an important trading centre, as much with the peoples of the north or of Africa as for the exchange with products from the Far East or Europe.

Istanbul's Grand Bazaar, in the old town, was originally built in the 11th century by Mehmet Fatih, the Conqueror, to serve as a cloth market The present bazaar was rebuilt in 1898.

Along the Greek coast

Opposite: Pella, north-west of Salonika, was the birth town and capital of Philip II of Macedonia, father of Alexander the Great.

The Greek mainland, on the side that faces the Cyclades and the Aegean Sea, has the promontory of Sounion as the foremost part of Attica, and when you round the cape, you find a port, and a temple of Athene Sounias on a hill on the promontory.

PAUSANIAS, *Description of Greece*

This temple was of the Doric order, and of a good period of architecture. I could make out in the distance the sea of the Archipelago, with all its islands: the setting sun tinged pink the coasts of Zea and the fourteen fine columns of white marble at the foot of which I had sat down. The sages and junipers gave forth an aromatic scent around the ruins, and the noise of the waves scarcely reached the point where I sat.

CHATEAUBRIAND, *Itinerary from Paris to Jerusalem*

Cape Sounion, the holy cape of Athens, mentioned in the Odyssey, was a dangerous place for shipping. Above, the Temple of Poseidon, built in the 5th century BC.

Page spread overleaf: The Acropolis at Athens, originally a fortress of the upper town, then the seat of political, administrative and military power, which would subsequently become the religious and spiritual centre of the city.

249

Arrival in Italy

Opposite: Brindisi, a port on the Ionian Sea, was linked to Rome by the Appian Way. Two columns marking the end of the Appian Way were erected here. Only one remains intact, decorated with twelve busts of Neptune, Jupiter, Juno, Amphitrite and some Tritons.

From everywhere by land and sea there comes to you that which the seasons harvest, that which the many countries, rivers, ponds, and craftsmen of the Greeks and Barbarians produce. If someone should need to see all the products of the world, he should travel the entire universe or come to your town, for all that grows, all that is made in every country, is always here in abundance. The laden ships bring these products here from everywhere, every year both in the high season and at the return of autumn. And the town is like a common market for the whole earth.

AELIUS ARISTIDES, *In Praise of Rome,* XXVI, 10 – 13

Ostia, a former port situated only 30 kilometres from Rome, saw a busy traffic despite its gradual sanding up, before being abandoned in favour of Centumcellae (Civitavecchia). Above, a detail from an Ostian mosaic.

Right: The Appian Way is bordered at intervals by funerary monuments.

The many moasics at Ostia (below) are a reminder of the great commercial activity of the port. The signs of the traders can still be seen here, as can the remains of the storehouses where the merchandise was stocked.

Trajan's Arch (centre right), at Benevento, was erected in AD 114 to celebrate the completion of the Trajan Way.

Roman roads (right and opposite) were paved with large stones placed on layers of cement and gravel. They usually followed a rectilinear course and one that was as level as possible, crossing valleys by means of imposing bridges. About four metres wide, the Appian Way, built in 312 BC, grew wider still as it drew near to Rome.

254

Venice, homeland of Marco Polo

All that remains today of the palace of the Polo family, nicknamed 'Milione' for the tales of fabulous riches that these merchants must have seen during the course of their journeys to the East.

Right: The Palace of the Doges, the seat of political power of the Most Serene Republic of Venice, which organised its commercial empire by setting up trading centres in Egypt, at Constantinople, in the eastern Mediterranean, and the Crimea.

Above: The door through the entrance to the Palace of the Doges, the 'Porta della Carta', the doge kneels before the winged lion of St. Mark, the city's patron saint. From the 12th century, the doge was elected for life by the oligarchy of aristocrats, and his authority became less and less influential until it was simply a symbol of the authority of the state.

From the mission of Gan Ying to the Roman Empire in AD 98, and that of the merchant known as the Envoy of the Emperor Antoninus in 166, no trace of any further mission anywhere was found in historic documents for several centuries. Nothing, that is, except a mention in AD 226 of the arrival of a merchant from Da Qin in the kingdom of Wu, one of the Three Kingdoms, into which China was divided in the 3rd century. This merchant, who had come via Tonking, is said to have arrived back in his country safe and sound, bringing with him some black dwarfs. There is also an account of a mission from Da Qin which is said to have brought to the emperor of China, in AD 284, 30,000 rolls of paper 'of a honey-like scent'. But this is almost certainly a fable: the tree with a scent of honey is the aloe, which grows especially in Annam. The mission would have had to buy aloe wood en route to present it to the emperor.

IDEAS AND THINGS

From then on until the 13th century — the time of the great missions of the pope and the king of France to the Mongol empire, and of the famous voyage made by Marco Polo — no account of any journey between the West and China has come down to us. Even so, during this period, both products and manufacturing methods were exchanged, and, above all, this route brought an exchange of ideas, carrying religions such as Nestorianism, Manicheism, Zoroastrianism, and especially Buddhism. It is precisely through Buddhist pilgrims that we possess evidence of the Silk Road, at least of that part of it that ran between India and China.

We have scant information regarding the ways and means by which Buddhism was introduced to China, and about the first translations into Chinese of Buddhist Sanskrit texts that had come from India or Central Asia, especially through Turkistan. Under the reign of Emperor Ming of the Han dynasty, in the 1st century AD, the first missionaries of whom we have record are Kasyapa Matanga and Dharmaratna, who are said to have been brought to the Yuezhi by a Chinese mission. But the first important translator mentioned in the tradition was a Parthian, An Shigao, who arrived at Luoyang in AD 148. In fact, most of the translators of the early years of the Christian era were not simply Indians, but Indo-Scythians such as Lokaksema, and Sogdians such as Kang Ju or Kang Mengxiang, who collaborated with An Shigao, as well as Kucheans such as Bo Yan, Khotanese such as Moksala, and so on.

The great Travellers

The first great traveller was the monk Faxian who went to India between AD 399 and 414. From Changan he made his way with four other monks to Dunhuang, then passed through Shanshan (Loulan), Yutian (Khotan) and Zihe (Karghalik), crossed the Congling Mountains (Pamirs), and so reached

Opposite: Caravans could simultaneously comprise camels, horses and donkeys, as illustrated (opposite) by this fragment of a wall painting on the Mount of the Five Terraces, Wutai Shan, in Dunhuang cave 61 (end of 10th century).

Yuhui (Tashkurgan). After that, his route is rather uncertain. He stayed at a place called Qiecha (which Chavannes thinks was Kashgar, and others Iskardu), and, via the Snow Mountains, he came to northern India. After staying in the kingdoms of Uddiyana and Gandhara, he proceeded along the valley of the Ganges and visited the main Buddhist sites there. He stayed for three years at Pataliputra, then two years at Tamralipti, before setting sail for Ceylon, and then for Java and China.

During this period, other monks made the journey to India. Shimeng, between AD 404 and 424, followed the same outward route as Faxian, but returned overland. Fayong set out in AD 420 with twenty other monks. He followed the route through northern Tarim, and passed through Turfan, Kucha and Kashgar before returning to China by sea after a stay in India.

A century later, between AD 518 and 522, Songyun made his way to Gandhara by the southern route, the one followed by Faxian.

But the pilgrim *par excellence* was Xuanzang (AD 602–664), one of the greatest translators of Buddhist texts, who undertook a lengthy excursion across India and Central Asia over fifteen years. Raised among learned teachers, Xuanzang, according to his hagiography, had astounded his fellow students by his knowledge and had acquired a certain fame. On discovering important divergences in the available texts, he decided to go to India itself in order to research the sources. He set out in AD 629. It was then forbidden for anyone at all to leave China without permission, and Xuanzang at first came up against the refusal of the authorities to let him go. He therefore set off alone and in secret along the northern Tarim route. On leaving the pass of the Jade Gate, Yumenguan, he was halted while passing a signal tower and was able to continue only by his great powers of conviction. After much difficulty, he crossed the Shifting Sands and came to Yiwu (Hami). Then, he passed through Gaochang (Turfan), where he was given a lavish welcome by the king. He resumed his journey with an escort, some equipment, some silks and some money, together with letters of introduction. He reached Aqini (Karashar), then Quzhi (Kucha), where he stayed for two months. He set off again with servants, horses and camels and tackled the crossing of the Ling Mountains (otherwise known as the Tien Shan) via the Bedel Pass, where more than ten of his companions died of cold, together with a number of horses and oxen. He came out by Lake Qingchi (Issyk-kul) with its greenish-black salt waters. At Suye (Tokmak), he met the Turkish khan, then he continued westwards through the Land of a Thousand Springs, passing through Daluosi (Talas), Zheshi (Tashkent) and Samojian (Samarkand), whose inhabitants practised the fire-cult, that is, Zoroastrianism. After that, Xuanzang made his way to Duheluo (Tukhara), after passing through the Iron Gates, so named because the narrow gorge here had a double gate on which small iron bells were hung. Xuanzang then turned off this route to go to Bohe (Balkh). There, he saw the relics of the Buddha, his wash-bowl, one of his teeth, and his broom. He then crossed the fearsome Snow Mountains, known as the Hindu Kush, and so came to Fanyanna (Bamiyan), where he admired the huge statues of the Buddha carved out of the cliff. He then made his way to Jinbishi (Kapisa, otherwise known as Begram), and finally came to Northern India, first to Lampaka, then to Gandhara, and then to Uddiyana. He visited the main Buddhist sites in the

He then entered the desert of sands, and guiding himself by the piles of bones and the mounds of horse droppings that he saw in the distance, he continued on his journey for a while at a slow and painful pace. Suddenly he saw several hundred armed troops who seemed to cover the plain. He saw them now march, now halt. All the soldiers were clad in felt cloths and furs. Here, there appeared richly accoutred camels and horses; there, sparkling spears and shining banners. Soon there were new shapes, new figures, and at every moment, this shifting scene offered a thousand metamorphoses. He looked in the distance, as far as his sight could discern it; but scarcely did he seem to draw near, than they vanished. At first glance, the Master of the Law seemed to have descried a multitude of brigands. But on seeing them disappear, at the very moment when he believed them close to him, he realised that they were idle images, created by the demons.

HUILI *and* YANZONG,
Biography of Xuanzang

The monk Xuanzang, a traveller par excellence, *is often shown walking with a book-rest on his back full of Buddhist texts and pictures.*

Ganges valley before venturing farther south to Dravidian country. From there, he travelled to the north and, on the return journey, again traversed the Hindu Kush with some difficulty: 'At this moment, there remains only seven priests, twenty servants, one elephant, ten donkeys, and four horses'. He then arrived at Qiepantuo (Khavanda) in the region of Tashkurgan, and set off from there for Qiasha (Kashgar) in the company of merchants. On the way, they were attacked and robbed by brigands. Xuanzang then followed the familiar southern route, passing through Zhuojujia (Karghalik), Jusadanna (Khotan), Nirang (Niya), Zhemoduona (Jumo, Cherchen), Nafubo (Loulan) and Shazhou (Dunhuang). From there, he addressed a plea to the emperor regarding the journey that he had undertaken in defiance of orders, and was welcomed in the capital with great honour. He brought with him relics, statues and a great number of sacred Buddhist texts, some 650 works in all. During the return journey, Xuanzang had lost a good many books when the elephant that was carrying them had drowned. But he had taken others from Kucha and Kashgar. The works that he managed to bring back to the capital were transported by twenty horses.

Until his death, Xuanzang took it upon himself to translate these texts, organising a sizeable team which employed a rigorous and technical system of translation. He also devoted part of his time to drawing up his 'Comments on the Lands of the West' *Xiyu Ji.*

Other pilgrims took the route to India in the 7th and 8th centuries, such as Wukong, between AD 751 and 790, who seems to have followed the southern route, and especially Yijing (AD 634–713), another great translator, who between AD 671 and 695 also went to India, but by boat. Without any doubt there were others who went there before the 10th century, but no accounts of their journeys have come down to us.

There was then a long hiatus in the tales of journeys made. With the exception of the 'Account of China and India', sometimes attributed to a merchant named Solaïman, an account compiled in the 9th century and based on the information of travellers (with the journeys made by Arabs usually undertaken by sea), it was only in the 13th century that new accounts provided us with further information.

At this time, the unification of nomadic peoples under the iron rule of Ghengis Khan (1167–1227) and the Mongol conquests as far as Russia gave a new importance to the old land-based silk route, superseded some time previously by the sea routes, especially as far as trade with the Arabs was concerned.

There were at once diplomatic, religious and commercial reasons which attracted western travellers to the road to China. Silk was no longer the sole vehicle of commercial exchange. Popes and kings, expecially Louis IX, were anxious to establish contact with the Mongols, as much with the aim of evangelisation as in the quest for an alliance against the Moslems.

In 1245, Pope Innocent IV sent four envoys to the East. Joannes de Plano Carpini, setting out from Lyon, travelled for fifteen months before coming to Karakorum, in the Orkhon valley, as bearer of a message from the pope. In his 'History of the Mongols', he detailed his route: Prague, Breslau, Krakow, Kiev, Kaniev, then along the north shore of the Caspian Sea and the Aral Sea, along

Several pictures of itinerant monks accompanied by a tiger have frequently been taken as representations of Xuanzang, despite the noticeable 'foreign' style of the figure. Whatever the case, these travelling monks seeking Buddhist texts or foreign missionaries seem to have made their journeys with the protection of the Baosheng tathagatha.

the valleys of the Syr Darya, the Zhu and the Ili, across Dzungaria and the Altai chain of mountains. Plano Carpini returned in 1247. Soon after, Louis IX sent André de Longjumeau to Mongolia in his turn. He set off from Nicosia on the island of Cyprus in 1249, and returned in 1251 without anyone knowing the result of his mission. Immediately after, it was William of Ruysbroeck, a Franciscan like Joannes de Plano Carpini, who left Constantinople to make his way also to Karakorum between 1253 and 1255, similarly through the Crimea.

Somewhat later, attempts were made to set up a residence in China for missionary bishops. The initiator was Jean de Montcorvin (1247 – 1328), who set off

This mountain (the Mountain of Ice) is very dangerous, and its summit reaches the sky. Since the beginning of the world, the snow has gathered here and has changed into blocks of ice which melt neither in spring nor in summer. Hard and shining ice-sheets stretch to infinity and merge with the clouds. If you turn your gaze to them, they dazzle with their brilliance. You find icy peaks which descend in slopes on either side of the route, with some a hundred feet high and others several dozen feet wide. It is thus difficult to cross the latter, and perilous to ascend the former. Add to this the gusts of wind and the whirlwinds of snow, with which you are assailed at every moment, in such a way that, even with shoes of double thickness and clothing protected by furs, you cannot prevent yourself from shivering with cold. When you wish to eat or sleep, you find no place where you can rest. You then have no other recourse than to hang up a cooking pot to prepare your food, or to lay matting on the ice to sleep.

HUILI *and* YANZONG,
Biography of Xuanzang

in 1289 for China, at first along the land route through Anatolia and the Caucasus, then by sea from Ormuz, making a stopover in India on the way. But he had no successor. Another Franciscan, Odoric de Pordenone, also went to China, between 1315 and 1330, travelling likewise mostly by the sea route.

Apart from these short-lived religious attempts, of whose first fruits the Jesuits would know nothing when they set sail for China at the end of the 16th

When Xuanzang returned to China, after more than fifteen years in travelling, he brought from India several hundred Buddhist works carried by an elephant. Opposite, a caravan with a white elephant, illustrating a passage from the Sutra of the Lotus in Dunhuang cave 103.

263

century, the routes to Asia were freely followed by merchants. The best known of these were undoubtedly the Polos. Between 1261 and 1265, Matteo and Niccolò Polo set off from Soldaia, a Venetian trading post in the Crimea, for the court of Kublai Khan, the Great Khan. Their route, given by Marco Polo in his *Description of the World,* is not very certain. It appears that they went through Sarai, capital of the Mongols of the Golden Horde, not far from present Volgograd, then came to Bukhara and Karakorum. The precise reasons for the journey undertaken by Matteo and Niccolò Polo remain unclear. Not much more is known about the motives for their second voyage of 1271, in which Marco Polo also took part. Nothing in the *Description* mentions any kind of commercial transaction. Instead, the three voyagers took letters from the Pope with them for Kublai Khan and oil from the lamp of the Holy Sepulchre. After staying at Acre, then at Laias, in the south of Asia Minor, the Polos set off for Khanbalik (Peking), Kublai Khan's new capital. Their route is difficult to follow, since Marco Polo mentions in his account both the places through which he passed and those that he had simply heard about as being close to his route. He probably went via Erzurum and Tabriz, then through the region of the Dry Tree to the south of the Caspian Sea (Khorassan?) and on towards Balkh, and after that continuing through Kashgar, Yarkand, Khotan, Lob (Charklik?), Suzhou (Jiuquan), Ganzhou (Zhangye), Ezina (Karakhoto) and Ergiuul (Liangzhou). He stayed for sixteen years in China in the service of the Mongol administrators, and did not return to Venice until 1295, by the sea route.

By contrast, at the same period, two Nestorian monks, born in China but of Turco-Mongol origin, decided to set out for the holy places of Jerusalem. Bearing instructions from Kublai Khan, whose mother belonged to the Nestorian faith, Rabban bar Sauma and Marqus left Khanbalik in about 1278, taking with them clothing that they were to dip in the Jordan and place on the Holy Sepulchre. They passed through Koshang, north-east of the great bend of the Yellow River, then through the Tangut capital (Ningxia), Khotan, Kashgar, Talas and Khorassan to arrive in Maragha. From there, they made their way to Baghdad, Mosul, Nisibin and Arbela, then to Ani in Armenia and on to Georgia to reach Jerusalem by sea. But as the routes were cut off, they were obliged to retrace their steps. It was then that Marqus became a Nestorian patriarch under the name of Mar Yaballaha III, while Rabban Sauma was appointed Visitor General. Arghun, the Mongol khan who reigned over Persia, would send him much later, in 1287, to Rome, then to Paris, where he took a letter to Philip the Fair, and to Gascony where he met the King of England before returning to Persia.

All these travel tales give us an insight into the traffic that passed to and fro along the Silk Road. They reveal the great variety of routes made down the ages. Equally, they reveal the intensity of the trade. They also give us a tantalising glimpse of those travellers who left us no account of their journey.

This period of intense traffic between Europe and China in the 13th and 14th centuries closes with the beginning of the Ming dynasty in China, in 1368, a dynasty that would remain for several centuries. Later, trade was undertaken almost exclusively by sea routes. This was the case, for example, for the voyages made by most of the Jesuit missionaries in the 16th and 17th centuries. The only exception was Beneditto Goës. He went from India to China between 1603 and

The Franciscan monk William of Ruysbroeck, sent by Louis IX, King of France, to the court of the Great Khan, set off from Constantinople to travel to Karakorum between 1253 and 1255 by a land route. He returned later to Europe after making a journey of about 17,000 kilometres.

1605 by an overland route, passing through Kabul, Kashgar, Aksu, Kucha, Turfan, Hami and Suzhou, where he died in 1607 without having finally reached Peking. Those travellers who still went by the land route were mainly Persians.

The Trade Routes

The accounts made by travellers are above all the accounts of envoys or pilgrims. The merchants did not write such accounts, although Marco Polo was an exception. It seems that, at least for the Italian merchants of the 13th century about whom we are reasonably well informed, they liked to disguise the aims and conditions of their movements. By good fortune, a trade manual such as that of Francesco Pegolotti, *La Praticha della Mercatura,* compiled in about 1340, tells us of the commercial practices that were followed at the beginning of the 14th century, in particular in Asia.

First, the handbook describes a route with great precision. Leaving from Tana on the Sea of Azov, after twenty-five days with a cart drawn by oxen, or after ten or twelve days with a horse-drawn cart, the traveller arrived at Gittarchan (Astrakhan). Then, after a day's journey by boat, he came to Sarai, on the Volga, and after a further eight days to Saracando (Saraichik in the Urals). This section of the journey could also be made overland, but the cost of transporting merchandise was less by boat. Then, twenty days were needed to reach Organci (Urgench) on the Amu Darya, south of the Aral Sea, with carts drawn by camels. From Urgench, an important caravan and trading centre, and famous for its organdie, the traveller made his way to Oltrarre (Otrar, north-west of Tashkent), taking thirty-five to forty days with the same kind of transport. But if he travelled without merchandise, he could go direct from Saracando to Oltrarre in only fifty days. From Oltrarre to Amalecco, near Yining in the Ili valley, the journey, made with pack-asses, took forty-five days. From there to Campicion (Ganzhou, present Jiuquan), another seventy days were needed with the donkeys, then forty-five days more on horseback to make Quinsay (Hangzhou). There, coin money could be exchanged for paper money. From Quinsay to Gamalecco (Khanbalik, otherwise Peking), was a further thirty days' journey.

Pegolotti also describes the conditions of the journey. At Tana, he needs to recruit a good interpreter and two servants who have a knowledge of Cuman (a Turco-Mongol dialect). The provisions to be taken are basically flour and salted fish, with other food obtainable en route. The cost of the journey is from sixty to eighty sums of silver (otherwise under a thousand florins of the day) for the journey to China with an interpreter, two servants, and merchandise with a value of twenty-five thousand gold florins. On the return journey, the outlay was at most about five sums of silver for each beast of burden. The load carried by an ox-drawn cart was ten Genoese kantars, or 470 kilos. A cart drawn by three camels could carry thirty kantars, or 1400 kilos. The horse-drawn carts, however, could take six and a half kantars of silk (305 kilos).

The route was, he said, perfectly safe, both by day and by night, except perhaps between Tana and Sarai, but the journey should be made in a group.

A pioneer traveller on the Silk Road, Marco Polo (1254 – 1324) accompanied his father and his uncle on their second journey to China, between 1271 and 1295. He would stay there more than fifteen years before returning by sea.

The best procedure was to take cloths on setting out, and to exchange them at Urgench for paper money. Silks could be brought back from China.

All the details in Pegolotti's handbook were provided by other merchants, as he himself had never travelled to China.

Later, at the beginning of the 17th century, another traveller, Beneditto Goës, a missionary to Cathay, joined a convoy of merchants in order to obtain entry to China, himself disguised as an Armenian merchant. Matteo Ricci and Nicolas Trigault, in their *History of the Christian Expedition to the Kingdom of China,* published in 1616, provide us with some details about his journey and the caravans. The latter were not always very frequent, and travelled between

SEA OF AZOV	TANA		ASTRAKHAN			URGENCH		TASHKENT	
	25 days with Oxen		9 days by boat		20 days with camel		35 to 40 days with camel		45 days wi

Lahore and Kashgar just once a year. More than five hundred people took to the road together, with horses, camels and carts. The route was not very safe, and the journey was frequently made at night. Beneditto Goës lost a dozen horses during the journey to Kashgar, as much from thieves as from fatigue and the poor roads. The caravan halted at Kashgar, and from there to China continued as another caravan. Sometimes there was not even a caravan every year, for it had to be certain that entry could be gained to the Chinese capital as well as to the country itself. In fact, under the Ming dynasty, which was when Goës made his journey, it seems that only foreigners with accreditation as envoys were admitted to China. This was why merchants would pass themselves off as envoys and would deliver gifts for the emperor to the Chinese authorities, taking these from the merchandise that they carried. Sayyid Ali Khitayi, a merchant from the region of Bukhara, describes this situation at the beginning of the 16th century, in his 'Account of China', *Khitay-nameh.* Two merchants out of ten were authorised to go to Peking, while the remainder had to wait at Ganzhou for the return of their colleagues. Both parties were provided with board and lodging by the Chinese. Once on Chinese territory, the merchants took on the status of official envoys and travelled via the posting stations, at each of which they found horses and carts, food and lodging, with the stations also used, especially, by messengers bearing orders. A century earlier, Ghiyath ed-Din, the envoy of Shah Rokh, the son and successor of Tamerlane, had already written approvingly of this system in his travel log.

The means of transport, as already revealed by Pegolotti, varied over the caravan routes, with the merchant using by turns for his merchandise either ox-drawn carts, horse-drawn carts, carts drawn by camels, or else pack-asses or pack-horses. The merchant himself could ride by horse or donkey or on any other mount that he chose. At that time, the merchandise itself was not always transported from one end to the other by the same merchants. Trading took place in the great caravan centres, and the caravans would frequently cover only a section of the total route.

Among the different animals used for transport, the horse was naturally the animal and mount that was most frequently encountered from one end of the Silk Road to the other, with its different races. Progress in the techniques of horse-drawn transport, and especially the introduction to Europe of the foot-

YINING   JIUQUAN   HANGZHOU

onkeys   70 days with donkeys   45 days on horseback

There were many kinds of transport depending on the merchandise as well as on the climate and the terrain of the regions travelled.

stirrup, and harness with breast- and collar-straps, considerably improved the transportation of people and property. Despite their relative commonness, horses were the object of particular attention from the Chinese, as in the time of the Han, and likewise from the Indians. Marco Polo describes horses several times in his writings, such as those of Badakshan, famous as racehorses who needed no horseshoes. There was also the well-known story of the horse brought from Italy by the papal legate Giovanni de Marignolli, in 1342, to be offered to the Mongol emperor of China. This great horse was so valued that its portrait was drawn.

The donkey had its advantages. It was less delicate and sturdier than the horse, less demanding, too, and less expensive, although slower. Marco Polo, again, wrote approvingly of the donkeys he had seen in Persia, which were so swift, so patient, so lively and so temperate by nature, as well as being such good beasts of burden, that they cost more than horses.

As one might expect, the camel is particularly valued for making desert crossings, especially along reasonably level routes. It can carry a heavier load than the horse, while still covering a distance of at least thirty-five kilometres a day. The camel has sometimes been credited with the ability of finding water: 'To the west of Dunhuang, you cross shifting sands, and over more than a thousand *li,* there is no water. It can happen that people are unable to find underground streams. But, if you ride a camel, this animal knows where the water runs. And when he arrives at such a place, he stops and refuses to go further, and with his foot he tramples the ground. The man then digs in the trampled place and he finds water' (*Bowu Zhi,* quoted in *Taiping Yulan,* 901).

The camel is in any case one of the most common means of transport, especially between Central China and Russian Turkistan. Contracts for the hiring of camels for journeys made in the 9th century, between Dunhuang and Turfan, have come down to us among the famous 'Dunhuang manuscripts'. These contracts were not for trading journeys, but for various types of personal missions. Here is the text of one such contract (more precisely a draft, or copy for a contract): 'The 22nd day of the 1st moon of the year *bingwu,* Song Chong (?), private individual of the canton of Hingrun, having to make a mission to Xizhou (Turfan) and needing a camel, has hired from So and So, private individual of the same canton, a male camel of eight years. They have agreed the price of (the

When the heat was too great, or in order to avoid robbers, the journey was sometimes made at night if the route permitted.

Tombs of the Tang dynasty have yielded many kinds of funerary statuettes featuring caravan merchants of a markedly foreign appearance. These were probably Sogdians.

hire of) this camel at one piece of raw silk (per month, from) the 1st moon (?); by the 7th moon, he must have supplied the complete price. If he has not supplied it by the time stated, there will be an imposition of interest in conformity with the customary regulations. If it should chance that the camel is wounded or lost during the journey, the cost of hiring remaining due (to the owner), the hirer must provide an identical camel. If any misfortune should befall the hirer in the course of his movements, it will be required for his son So and So to provide an identical camel, deducting this from the cost of hiring. If the beast falls ill and dies (on the journey), three of his travelling companions must give witness of this ...' (Pelliot Chinese ms 2652).

Among the beasts of burden, mention should also be made of the ox. Although it is a slower animal than the horse, it can carry much heavier loads. Marco Polo describes, for example, the oxen in the Reobar region, no doubt in southern Iran, as very large and very strong beasts which lie down like camels to be loaded. He also describes the enormous oxen, the yaks, which he saw in the region of Xining, in the present province of Gansu. He brought back to Venice some of their extraordinary long hair.

The carts that were drawn by horses or camels, or even oxen, could cover stages of the journey as long as those covered by the pack-animals, only more slowly. The convoys would stop daily at halting places along the routes, such places being square courtyards surrounded by a few rooms where travellers could find water from a well, hay, straw, grain, and poultry. They were sometimes merely simple shelters. At greater intervals, and situated in towns and villages, were the caravanserais, which served as staging posts for the travellers and as trading places. These huge rectangular courtyards were surrounded by a gallery with rooms facing onto it, and they were places where travellers could buy all that they needed.

Thanks to such methods of conveyance, the merchandise was transported in different directions. Silk had long been the main objective of journeys made by western merchants, even if it was not the sole commodity in the transactions with China when silk manufacture was developed in the Middle East and then in Europe itself. In the 13th century, it frequently happened, in fact, that the silk imported to Italy by the Genoese and the Venetians came not from China but from Turkistan, Iran, or the Caucasus. In the 14th century, Chinese silk was sold even more cheaply than silk from Turkistan and the Caucasus. It may not have

In Dunhuang cave 45, a painting of the Tang era, illustrating the Sutra of the Lotus, shows an episode in which foreign merchants are being attacked and robbed of their baggage by brigands of Chinese appearance.

been valued so highly, it is true, but it was after all more plentiful and very likely less expensive in its place of origin. According to Pegolotti, the resale price of silk in Genoa was three times what had been paid for it in China. In deducting the cost of transport, estimated at half the purchase price, there remained a one hundred percent profit, without including the cost of the outward journey.

This is why it was important not to set off empty-handed. Among the products of exchange, since the earliest times, the horse has always occupied an important place, as we have seen. But textiles, fabrics and woollen goods were

Xuanzang describes several such attacks. In northern India, he was himself attacked and robbed of his clothes and provisions by about fifty brigands. Near Karashar, he saw the corpses of several dozen merchants who had been assailed by robbers.

also appreciated. In 1303, a trilingual commercial glossary, Latin-Persian-Cuman, mentions more than a dozen types of fabric with their place of origin, as well as giving the standard commercial terms.

Other goods were also transported by the merchants to China, whether from their place of origin, or purchased en route, such as amber or crystal, taken by the Polos. Much of what was transported was gifts for the Great Khan rather than merchandise proper, such as the tortoiseshell or rhinoceros horn that served as gifts under the Han. Even so, many other kinds of goods were taken to China. Above all they were substances that were useful in medicine or pharmacy, or for dietary purposes, even as drugs of immortality. From Persia and India came coriander, cloves, sandalwood, nutmeg, cubeb, cardamom, myrrh, sugar cane and mastic, as well as camphor and aloes, used for funeral rites, all these being products brought by the Sogdians, then the Persians, on overland routes, or by the Arabs by sea. There was also lapis lazuli and indigo, used as cosmetics for the eyelids and eyebrows, henna, used for varnishing the nails, as well as incense and the mysterious ambergris — a secretion from the intestines of the sperm-whale which was said to originate from dragon's spittle in China and was regarded as an excrement in the West. Amianthus, too, had caused a sensation from the times of the Han dynasty, and was long thought to be produced by the fur of the salamander-rat.

Diamonds, pearls, coral and glass also came to China. The diamond was not granted the same high status that it was in the West, as the Chinese regarded it more as a cutting or piercing tool than as a precious stone. Glass objects had long been traded, originally in the Roman Empire, then by the Sogdians. In the 5th century, the Sogdians taught the Chinese how to manufacture a glass that was a brilliant as that of the West, but this did not in fact interrupt the importing of glass objects, at least until the invention of porcelain.

Jade, produced chiefly in the region of Khotan, occupied a specially important place in the exchanges between Central Asia and China. It was always greatly valued for making ornaments and emblems of power. Thus, Beneditto Goës supplied himself with jade at Khotan to facilitate his arrival in China as a merchant, since 'there was no greater nor more frequent trading' than in jade.

For her part, China exported only silk, even if this was the basis of commercial negotiations. Musk was particularly sought after in China, and even more so in Tibet. Spices and drugs such as ginger, ginseng, rhubarb, jujube, curcuma and cinnamon were the objects of transactions with the West. Tea, of course, would reach Arab countries by sea and Russia by overland caravan.

Foreign merchants arriving in China under the Tang dynasty were all branded as 'barbarians', hu, whatever their origin. Their clothes, hairstyles and faces were the source of much wonderment.

The Religious Routes

The routes that allowed the passage of merchandise and the passing on of manufacturing techniques were equally favourable for the communication and diffusion of ideas, especially religious ideas.

Buddhism, born in India, was the foreign religion which had the greatest impact on China, more so than Manicheism, Islam, Zoroastrianism or Nestorianism. Buddhism spread to the north-west and reached Central Asia, more especially Bactriana and Sogdiana, then extended east following the Silk Road, transported by merchant caravans. At the same time, it also spread to Indonesia and the Philippines and South-East Asia generally by the sea route.

In Central Asia, Buddhism flourished especially at Khotan, where in AD 211 the first monastery is said to have been founded. The coming of Buddhism to Khotan is thus founded on legend. According to what the pilgrim Xuanzang tells, a saint named Vairocana made his way from Kashmir to Khotan, where he persuaded the king to found a convent in which a statue of the Buddha appeared. From then on, the king took it upon himself to spread the teaching of the Buddha, that of the Great Vehicle. What is certain is that in 1892 Dutreuil de Rhins and Grenard discovered a manuscript in Kharoshti or Arameo-Indian writing, with Buddhist stanzas that appear to date from the 2nd century AD and which testify to the existence of Buddhism at Khotan during this period.

We are not well informed on the introduction of Buddhism to the other oases of Central Asia and Xinjiang. At Kucha, it is thought that Buddhism was known, if not practised, in the 1st century AD, but precise evidence relating to this is not found much before the 3rd century. It appears that Buddhism of the Little Vehicle predominated at Kucha. This preached personal salvation, whereas Khotan was an important centre for the propagation of the Great Vehicle, under which all human beings could attain the status of buddha.

The arrival of Buddhism in China remains mysterious. Tradition claims that the Emperor Ming of the Han (reigned AD 58 – 75) saw the Buddha in a dream and sent envoys to the Yuezhi (or to India) to learn about his teaching. They are said to have returned with Buddhist monks as well as books and statues. These books and statues are said to have been placed in the newly built Monastery of the White Horse. But this story was probably invented only towards the end of the 2nd century, and the Monastery of the White Horse is attested only at the end of the 3rd century.

If it has not been established that Buddhism was indeed active in China before the 2nd century AD, several texts seem to indicate that it was seminally present in the 1st century. This is what is inferred from the contents of an amnesty order of AD 65, mentioning the sacrifices that were fitting for the Buddha and the aid given to the Buddhist community for its food. This community, certainly one of foreigners or of people of foreign origin, had been established at Pengcheng, in the present province of Jiangsu. Indeed, these early traces show a Buddhism that was intimately blended with Taoism. The king of Chu, who was a beneficiary of this amnesty, sacrificed as much to the Buddha as to Huang-Lao, the Old Yellow One, an amalgam of Laozi (Lao-tseu) deified and of Huangdi, the Yellow Emperor, patron of magic, drugs and Taoist techniques.

Above: Manuscript on wooden boards in the Kharoshti script. Below: Fragment of a Buddhist scroll in Chinese written in the Tang dynasty (AD 618 – 907).

271

In its early period, Chinese Buddhism was moreover imbued with Taoism, with the translation of specifically Sanskrit terms borrowed largely from Taoism. In fact, Buddhism, as a religion so different in concept from those that had hitherto been practised in China, must have offered a familiar appeal. If it was unable to satisfy the adepts of Confucianism that dominated China under the Han, it would have pleased the Taoists despite their fundamental differences. By presenting a basic moral teaching and meditation techniques without evoking root notions that would have offended believers, Buddhist missionaries obtained a success that could only increase. Its practices, much gentler than those that had evolved in Taoism, could do nothing but attract. It was believed that the Buddha was none other than Laozi, who set out for the West to preach his teaching to the barbarians. More precise indications of the establishment of Buddhism in China are given to us by the ceremonies paid to the Buddha by the Emperor Huan (AD 147–167) in AD 166, but especially on the appearance in Luoyang of the first teams of translators. The best known of these translators was An Shigao, whose patronym refers to the land of Anxi, that is, Arsak, and thus denotes his Parthian origin. An all too beguiling legend tells how he was a prince who renounced his throne to enter the religious life. In reality, nothing is known of his life except the fact that he arrived in Luoyang in AD 148.

Buddhism, imported by foreigners, spread first and foremost among immigrant families settled in China, merchants, envoys, hostages, and the like. Several examples bear witness to this, such as that of An Xuan, a merchant and, like An Shigao, a Parthian, who came to Luoyang in AD 181, was converted, and entered his compatriot's community. The case of Zhi Qian (died c. AD 255), Qian the (Yue-)zhi, is different. His family had settled in China from the time of his grandfather. The great translator Dharmaraksa (Zhu Fahu, in Chinese, died AD 310), was also born, in about AD 230, into a family of *yuezhi* origin, at Dunhuang. Zhu Shulan, another translator of the end of the 3rd century, and likewise born in China in Henan, was of Indian origin. One could quote many more such instances.

Conversely, the spread of Buddhism was perhaps also favoured by those Chinese who held civil or military posts in Central Asia, even if no noteworthy mention of this remains.

The development of Buddhism in China certainly owed much to those who sought Buddhist texts in Central Asia, then in India. The first known traveller (who left no account of his journey) was Zhu Shixing who, dissatisfied with the version of the 'perfection of Gnosis' (*Prajnaparamita*) available at Luoyang, decided to go in search of the complete text. In AD 260, it would seem, he went to Khotan where he had the complete Sanskrit version copied. The copy was brought back by one of his disciples, who himself stayed in Khotan and died there. After him, there were numerous comings and goings among pilgrims, or more precisely among the 'Seekers of the Law'.

The traces left on the Silk Road by Buddhism are numerous, as indicated by archaeological discoveries made at the beginning of this century. Its influence is shown by the ruined stupas found at Miran, Niya and Loulan, which can be dated from the 3rd century. The carved or painted caves which mark out the var-

In the 7th century, Indian monks introduced to China a new form of Buddhism influenced by Tantrism. Its key features included mantras, or magic formulas, mudras, or ritual gestures, and the symbolic figures that comprised the mandala. This form of Buddhism, which would be ousted by Chan (Zen, in Japanese), obtained a more lasting hold in Tibet than it did in China. Here, a mandala figure of the Diamond Plan, one of the two great mandalas of esoteric Buddhism.

ious routes, at Kizil and Kumtura near Kucha, at Bezeklik and Toyuk near Turfan, at Mogao and Yulin near Dunhuang, at Biblingsi near Landzhou, and at Maijishan, are a powerful witness to its stamp on the very heart of China.

By contrast, one has to wonder why Buddhism never took root in a westerly direction. It is not possible to explain this meaningfully. Transported by merchants it could equally well have spread to the Middle East and Europe, as Brahmanism did, in a rather ineffectual way, to the Roman Empire. The mystery remains unsolved.

Other religions also made their way from west to east. First, because its traces are still firmly evident in China, was Nestorianism. The Nestorian Church, or more exactly the Chaldean Church, which had developed in Mesopotamia and Persia and which had broken with the Western Church in the 5th century, spread to Central Asia and eventually on to China. The history of its introduction is known to us from the famous stele of Xian erected in AD 781. This stele, which has caused much ink to flow, was disinterred in 1623 or 1625 during the construction of terraces not far from Xian, on the site of the former Tang capital, Changan, at the very spot where it had been erected. At the beginning of the 20th century, it was taken to the Forest of Steles at Xian. The stele, of 'the propagation of the radiant religion of Da Qin in the Middle Empire', contains on its main face a Chinese text that is both dogmatic and historic, surmounted by the title and by a Nestorian cross. Below and in the margins are inscriptions in Syriac, while the lateral faces give the names of members of the clergy in Syriac and Chinese. According to the Chinese text, it was one Aluoben who, in AD 635, arrived in Changan, bearing the 'True Scriptures'. The Emperor Taizong (reigned AD 627 – 649), on having these texts translated to learn their contents allowed him to propagate his teaching. And in AD 638, as the result of an imperial edict, a 'monastery of Da Qin' was built where twenty-one priests took up residence. The text adds that under the reign of Gaozong (AD 650 – 683), monasteries were founded in every prefecture. Nestorianism must then have met with varied fortunes until the great proscription of AD 845, which hit Buddhism as much as the other religions. It was perhaps at this time that the stele was buried. Other documents, apparently from the same period, attest the presence of Nestorianism in China, for example in the 'Hymn to the Holy Trinity', a Chinese translation of the Syriac version of the *Gloria in excelsis deo,* discovered by Paul Pelliot in the cave of manuscripts at Mogao near Dunhuang in 1908. This manuscript (Pelliot Chinese ms 3847) perhaps dates from the 8th century. A few other Nestorian manuscripts in Chinese, such as the 'Sutra of the Messiah Jesus', were similarly found at Dunhuang. Chinese Nestorian source are hardly forthcoming about the activity of the Nestorians, but in AD 845, when the order was made to destroy the Buddhist monasteries and those of the other religions, the Nestorian and Zorostrian monasteries, according to the text of the imperial edict, housed over three thousand people. Even so, that is a long way from the 260,500 Buddhist monks and nuns who were then sent into the secular world. Nestorianism did not survive in China, although it did in Central Asia. It took on a new life, however, at the time of the Mongol domination, since it had gained a hold on the court and family of Genghis Khan and was protected and even encouraged by Kublai Khan.

Several of the non-Chinese populations of Central Asia were also converted to Buddhism. This applied to the Tanguts, who founded a kingdom in the region now occupied by the provinces of Ningxia and Gansu. Above, a stupa in the ruins of their capital, Karakhoto.

The famous so-called Xianfu stele, raised in AD 781 near Changan, is now in the 'Forest of Steles' at Xian. Its inscriptions reveal the history of the introduction of Nestorian Christianity to China in the 7th century.

At the time when Nestorianism had been proscribed, in AD 845, Zoroastrianism, or Mazdaism, had been equally affected. Originating in Iran and established as the official religion of Sassanid Persia, Zoroastrianism was known in China under the name of the religion of the 'celestial god of fire'. Although none of its monuments have survived, a few rare references lead one to suppose that the religion had only a moderate development. Under the Tang, an imperial administrative office was charged with the management of its affairs, and it is known that several sanctuaries existed at Changan and Luoyang, as well as Dunhuang. Nevertheless, the cultural concepts and practices brought by Zoroastrianism were perhaps too foreign to Chinese ideas to be adopted.

By contrast, Manicheism, of more recent foundation, met with a certain amount of success, despite its dualism. Introduced into China towards the end of the 7th century, it was rapidly accepted, thanks to a skilful blend of Buddhist and Taoist concepts, with Laozi and Sakyamuni becoming the precursors of Mani, and it was then known as the 'Religion of Light'. In AD 731, a 'Catechism of the Religion of the Buddha of Light Mani' was even compiled on the order of the emperor. Its text was found among the Dunhuang manuscripts in two matching fragments, of which one is now preserved in London (Stein 3939) and the other in Paris (Pelliot Chinese ms 3884). Although the appropriation of the Buddha by the Manicheans was immediately condemned, its religious practices were not forbidden to foreigners living in China. But, in AD 843, Manicheism was proscribed before even the other religions. It would reappear fairly discreetly during the 14th century. But it was due to the Turks, from 763 onwards that it became the official religion of the kingdom of Uigur Turks that was set up in Mongolia and Chinese Turkistan (AD 744 – 840). Several traces of it have remained, especially in the region of Turfan, where at the beginning of the 20th century texts in Iranian languages (including Sogdian), Uigur Turkish and Chinese were found, as well as a number of paintings illustrating the manuscripts, mainly at Gaochang (Kocho, Karakhoja).

Islam, too, gained a foothold in China, although somewhat later. Founded in the 7th century, it spread west and east like wildfire. Thus, the Moslems took possession of Persia in the middle of the 7th century, before being checked in their conquest of Transoxiana (Tashkent region) at the beginning of the 8th century, but not before reaching Kashgar and then Turfan. The Chinese counterattack, which initially had some success in Turkistan, under the leadership of the Korean general Gao Xianzhi, was finally brought to a halt by the battle at Talas in AD 751. If this battle marked the end of Chinese domination over Turkistan, it also coincided with the retreat of the Moslems, due mainly to the decline and fall of the Omayyad caliphs. Islam took root in China in AD 755, perhaps as the result of the revolt of An Lushan, when the Uigurs, with Arab support, managed to gain the upper hand over the imperial troops and bring the rebellion to an end. The spread of Islam was especially slow in northern China, even though it eventually gained a considerable footing there. But Islam had also penetrated into southern China, thanks to the maritime trade, and in particular to Canton, where in the 9th century it is known that there was a representative of the Moslem community responsible to the Chinese authorities. The area reserved for Moslems was also mentioned by Ibn Battuta, in the middle of the 14th century.

This fragment of a page from a Manichean book, discovered at Gaochang (Kocho), near Turfan, and dating from the 8th or 9th century, shows seven elect with a calamus and a specimen of writing. The scroll is written in Sogdian.

Finally, Judaism was also introduced in China, having entered by the Silk Road, although traces of it are difficult to establish. With the exception of a small fragment in Hebrew discovered by Pelliot at Dunhuang, and another Judaeo-Persian fragment found at Dandan-oilik, near Khotan, by Aurel Stein, nothing has been preserved of the presence of Jews in China before the 12th century and the founding of the synagogue at Kaifeng.

Islam made only slow advances in China, but it has kept its foothold there to this day, especially in Xinjiang, where it is not only very active but even increasing. Friday afternoon prayers at Turfan, Urumqi, Kashbar or Khotan (shown here) gather many of the zealous faithful.

Art and Fashion

The Silk Road, as a channel for merchandise and ideas, was also the medium by which forms, styles, fashions and usages similarly travelled. There is no need to return to the coalescence of Graeco-Buddhic art generally found in Gandhara. However, emphasis should be placed on the transformations it underwent upon the spread of Buddhism to Central Asia and China. Central Asia, as the melting pot of different civilisations, was also the point of departure of stylistic influences on the art of Central China. Since the great discoveries of the archaeological missions of the beginning of the 20th century, art historians have become involved in the task of researching Indian, Kushan, Iranian, Syrian and other influences on the paintings and sculptures of Miran, Bamiyan, Kucha, Penzhikent, Khotan, Turfan and Dunhuang. The artistic shifts that have affected divinities such as Avalokiesvara, who is feminised

276

in China and known under the name of Guanyin, or again Vaisravana-Kubera, as much in their iconography as in their functions are entirely representative of the many influences that have permeated over the course of time thanks to the Silk Road. The arrival in China of original painters from Central Asia, such as Weichi Bozhina or Weichi Yiseng, who were born at Khotan, also had an effect.

The influence of the traffic of people and property on the Silk Road was particularly noticeable in China under the Tang dynasty, when a veritable infatuation for everything Persian or Turkish was rife among the Chinese. One proof of this, for exmaple, are the ornamental designs on fabrics showing animals facing each other. This was a fashion which affected all aspects of daily life in the capitals, such as clothing, cooking, music, etc. 'Inside the palace, Persian music is rated highly, while Persian food is served at the tables of the gentry and women vie with one another to wear Persian clothes'. This enthusiasm for the exotic led even Prince Li Chengqian, son of the Emperor Taizong, to dress in the Turkish manner, to speak Turkish rather than Chinese, and to set up a Turkish encampment within the very walls of the palace. At Changan, Persian cakes were greatly in favour. Clothes, make-up and hair-styles in the Persian or Turkish fashion were all the rage in the reign of Xuanzong (AD 712 – 756), and doubtless bewitched the famous concubine Yang Guifei.

The defeat of the Sassanids, who were conquered by the Moslems in AD 651, had led Prince Peroz to seek refuge in the Chinese court, and then to set himself up on the western borders of China in a endeavour, albeit unsuccessful, to restore the fallen dynasty. A person of foreign origin who was influential at court, as was An Lushan, could also play a part in the adoption of these exotic tastes. An Lushan, who became the favourite of the Emperor Xuanzong, was probably of Sogdian origin, with his personal name being a transcription of Roxane.

Among the artistic fashions of Central Asian inspiration that then developed in the Chinese capitals, music and dance occupied a special place. The music of Kocho, Kashgar, Bukhara and Samarkand, and also of India, was played by orchestras from these respective regions with their own instruments: flutes and mouth organs, percussion (gongs and drums) and stringed instruments, harps or lutes, of which the pipa, of Iranian origin, is the best known, since it remained in China and was introduced to Japan. The music of Kucha seems to have been the most popular.

Characters with bowls and birds. Scene from a Khotanese legend. Wooden board. Dandan-oilik. 7th century.

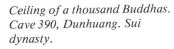

Ceiling of a thousand Buddhas. Cave 390, Dunhuang. Sui dynasty.

Buddha. Cave 37, Bezeklik.

Bodhisattva. Cave 45, Dunhuang. Tang dynasty.

Apsara playing the pipa. Cave 8, Kizil.

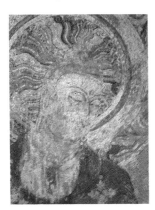

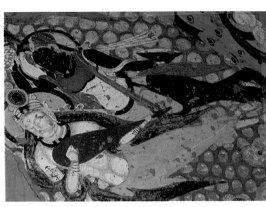

277

Conversion of the yaksa Atavika. Sikri stupa. Lahore Museum. Right: Statue of the Buddha. Gandhara.

Buddha preaching the Law. Gandhara. Peshawar Museum.

Mandala of the Diamond Plan. Alchi Gompa. Ladak.

Bas-relief at the Palace of Xerxes. Persepolis.

Men and women dancers, acrobats and conjurors enjoyed great success. There are several examples of these orchestras and dancing girls in the terracotta figurines discovered in tombs dating from the Tang dynasty. It was probably in the 7th century, too, that puppet shows, of Turkistani origin, took place for the first time in China. In the taverns of Changan or Luoyang, wines from grapes imported chiefly from Liangzhou, the present Gansu, were served in amber or agate goblets by ravishing serving girls of Sogdian or Tokharian origin, as described many times by poets of the Tang dynasty. The game of polo was also a sport imported from Persia at the beginning of the Tang period. This was highly popular at court, as much among women as men.

Many other examples could be given. But through these illustrations of religious, technical, commercial or artistic exchanges, we have evidence of the significant interchange between East and West that took place over the complex of commercial routes that have come to be known as the Silk Road. The influences of Central Asia on the Far East are still felt today, if not in China itself, then at least in Japan. As a consequence of the close relations maintained by Japan with China in the Tang period, several traces of these influences still exist there, with the objects, instruments and textiles preserved at the famous Shoso-in, the depository of treasure from the Todaiji temple at Nara, and also more diffuse influences, such as music, especially the music of the court, *gagaku*.

Right: Ubal, daughter of Jabal. Hatra.

The sun god. Hatra. Mosul Museum.

Right: Anthropomorphic ossuary. Koy-Krylgan-Kala, Khorezm. 1st century.

Impression from a seal, 2nd century. Baghdad Museum.

Masjid-i-Shah. Ispahan. 17th century.

Illustration of a paradise of Amitabha. Musicians and dancers decorate the lower part of the painting. Their instruments are frequently of Central Asian origin. Cave 112, Dunhuang. Tang dynasty.

The art of the mosaic, which is restricted to the Graeco-Roman and Byzantine Mediterranean, was at its height in Byzantium. Christ is depicted in the galleries of St. Sophia. Istanbul.

Balbal, or man carved from stone in a Turkish tomb. Kirghizia.

Horses and deer engraved in the rock. Ferghana.

Harp player. Pendzhikent. 7th – 8th centuries.

Anthropomorphic cover of a Sogdian ossuary.

THE SILK ROAD REDISCOVERED

The Silk Road had completely lost its role as a link between the West and China from the beginning of the Ming dynasty in 1368. This was for several reasons relating as much to the closure of China (for a short period only) as to the obstacles raised in the West in about the middle of the 14th century which restricted trade to establishments on the Black Sea coast.

China under the Ming was not entirely closed off, as contacts were frequent with Persia and Russia. But above

kingdoms of Central Asia from 1850 by Russia, who installed protectorates, or simply made annexations, in Khiva, Bukhara and Khokand, coupled with the designs that the British had on Turkistan from their possessions in India. The topographical research and observation of potential enemies that such exploration involved was not insignificant.

One of the chief English travellers to collect geographical information at this time was William Johnson, who in 1865 made his way to Khokand from Leh. The missions of Douglas Forsyth in the region of Kashgar in 1869 and 1873 had a more political motive. Among the many explorers who were active in Turkistan during this period, the most famous was undoubtedly the Russian, Nikolai M. Przhevalsky (1837 – 1888), who undertook four expeditions to this

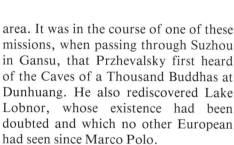

Left to right: Paul Pelliot; the keeper of the caves at Dunhuang, Wang Yuanlu; Langdon Warner; P.K. Kozlov; Sven Hedin at study, and in explorer's gear; Otani Kozui; Joseph Hackin.

all, the sea routes underwent a important phase of development, both from the West and from China, and this reduced the caravan routes to limited exchanges. Gradually, the great commercial exchanges of the past were obliterated from the Western public mind, and the revival of these remote contacts did not come about until the end of the 19th century, when there was a great deal of explorational activity in Turkistan. At the forefront was geographical exploration, carried out by the Russians, or from India by the English, then archaeological exploration, which involved the majority of the larger modern nations.

The source of this geographical exploration was the conquest of the

area. It was in the course of one of these missions, when passing through Suzhou in Gansu, that Przhevalsky first heard of the Caves of a Thousand Buddhas at Dunhuang. He also rediscovered Lake Lobnor, whose existence had been doubted and which no other European had seen since Marco Polo.

Among the various cartographical, geological, astronomical, meteorological and zoological operations that he carried out, Przhevalsky noted the presence of a breed of wild horse peculiar to the Altyn Tagh mountain chain. This 'Przhevalsky's horse' became very famous, and in applying Darwin's theories it was possible to see it as the original horse from which others must have directly descended. Circuses took an interest in the horse until it was observed that the particular breed was not as exotic as had been at first supposed. From a geographical point of view, explorers were intrigued by the Turfan Depression, especially as the irrigation system operating there by means of underground channels, the *karez,* was similar to that found in Iran.

Towards the end of the 19th century, geographical exploration, which was sometimes tinged with a political or military motive, was joined by a number of archaeological ventures. For example, on the expedition made by Captain Bower in 1889, the latter had gone in search of the murderer of Andrew Dalgleish, another explorer, also a merchant, who had been killed the previous year in the Karakorum Pass. While Bower was staying in Kucha, a Turk told him of an excavated town nearby, where

1890 to 1893, their ill-fated mission, in which Dutreuil de Rhins met his death, resulted in the acquisition of several manuscripts in Brahmi or Kharoshto script dating from the 6th and 7th centuries.

Archaeological enthusiasm gradually grew. In 1892, the Littledale couple, searching for specimens of wild camels, stopped at Kucha and discovered the caves subsequently known as the 'Caves of a Thousand Buddhas'. In 1894, Piotr K. Kozlov visited the 'Caves of a Thousand Buddhas' at Dunhuang, and noticed that many statues had been mutilated during the recent Moslem rebellion. The following year, the Swede Sven Hedin (1865–1952) began to add his contributions to the activity, and not only collected several manuscript fragments from the region of Khotan, but thanks to the account of his journey

its course until it disappeared in the desert sands, passing close to the ruins of Karadong, another excavated city. After that he returned to Khotan and from there made his way to Tibet.

The collection of documents and objects soon gathered pace. In 1898, Dimitri Klementz visited the ruins of Karakhoja (in Chinese Gaochang), Astana and Yarkhoto (in Chinese Jiaohe), near Turfan. After examining 130 caves, he took specimens of wall paintings, gathered manuscripts in Chinese and Sanskrit, and also took a number of photographs which would excite and interest the academic world. In 1899, Charles-Etienne Bonin, who had set out to trace the old Silk Road, departed from Peking for Ningxia, crossed the province of Gansu, and reached Urumji and Samarkand. From his journey, he

the only treasure he had found had been an old book, which he showed Bower. The Turk's find was actually several pages of Sanskrit in Brahmi script, written on birch bark, which on inspection appeared to date from the 5th century. On being sent to Calcutta, the Bower manuscript attracted the attention of the Indianist scholar Rudolph Hoernle, who deciphered it. This discovery unleashed a race between the Russians and the English to seek out more objects and manuscripts. The respective diplomatic representatives at Kashgar, Nikolai Petrovsky for the Russians, and George Macartney for the English, encouraged the search. The French joined in, also, with Dutreuil de Rhins and Fernand Grenard. Between

made the Turkistan explorations much better known. Sven Hedin had originally been interested in Iran. In 1895, he set out from Kashgar and pushed east into the Takla Makan Desert in the direction of Merket on the Yarkand river, nearly dying of thirst there but finally reaching the Khotan river. In December of that year he set out once more from Kashgar for Khotan, having heard that treasure-seekers had made some finds in a ruined village named Borasan (Yotkan). Sven Hedin discovered the remains of an excavated town which he called Taklamakan (Dandan-oilik) and conducted some brief digs there. In the wall paintings he examined, he noticed Indian, Greek and Persian influences. He then reached the Keriya Darya, and followed

brought back in particular some cast impressions which would be studied by Edouard Chavannes. The same year, Sven Hedin made his third expedition, financed by the King of Sweden. His aim was to descend the Yarkand river by boat, and then the Tarim river as far as Lobnor. As it was winter, and the river was frozen over, Hedin explored the desert to the south, going as far as the oasis of Cherchen. He then discovered Loulan, the former Chinese garrison abandoned in the 3rd century AD. From there he collected 36 manuscripts on paper of this period, and a further 120 on wood. That same year, 1899, the 12th International Congress of Orientalists was held in Rome. Hoernle and Radlov made their reports there on the archaeological discoveries in Turkistan. Among the manuscripts collected in the region of Khotan and sent to Hoernle by the British diplomatic agent Macartney, there were texts in extinct languages, in writing that would be deciphered by Hoernle. But the collection also happened to include a good number of manuscripts and xylographs in a language and script that were entirely unknown. These were discovered by one Islam Akhun, a treasure-seeker who had acted as Macartney's catering agent in Kashgar. Although several doubts were soon expressed, the manuscripts and xylographs were admitted as authentic by Hoernle. Soon after, at the time of his first expedition, Aurel Stein correctly accounted for these 'forgeries', which had been a complete invention on the part of their deviser, Islam Akhun.

After that he went to Karadong, still in the footsteps of Sven Hedin, but his excavations there were not fruitful. After returning to Kashgar, he set off for London with his gleaning of discoveries which would be deposited in the British Museum.

Shortly after, in 1902–1903, the first Japanese expedition was initiated by Otani Kozui, who when in England had heard of the finds made by Aurel Stein. Almost as soon as he arrived in Turkistan, Otani had to return to Japan, and he left in his place two assistants who devoted most of their attention to the sites of Kucha, from where they brought a number of archaeological items. The first German expedition also took place at this time, spurred by the revelations of the congress of Orientalists in 1899. It was led by Albert Grün-

stroyed by bombing in the Second World War.

The third German expedition immediately followed the second, since it began with the arrival of Grünwedel in Kashgar, where he joined Le Coq in December 1905. They explored Tumshuk, then Kumtura and Kizil near Kucha, Sorchuk near Karashar, and also Turfan.

In 1906–7, Aurel Stein made his second expedition, financed by the British Museum and the Government of India. Stein first explored the sites at Domoko and Rawak, in the region of Khotan, then Niya, where he found further manuscripts and textiles, and also Miran, where he found manuscripts in Tibetan. At Loulan, he unearthed several manuscripts on paper and wood, the majority in Chinese, dating from the

Aurel Stein (1862–1943), a Hungarian in origin, undertook his first expedition in 1900–1901, sponsored by Lord Curzon, Viceroy of India. He set off from Srinagar for Kashgar, and from there for Khotan. He began his excavations at Dandan-oilik, where Sven Hedin had spent some time earlier. There he discovered wall paintings and sculptures as well as Sanskrit manuscripts in Brahmi script and others in an unknown language which turned out to be Khotanese. He also found Chinese documents, including petitions, reports and contracts dating from the 8th century. He then made his way to Niya, where in one place alone he found 85 wooden tablets inscribed in Kharosthi.

wedel (1865–1935), in charge of the Indian Section at the Berlin Ethnological Museum. His objective was basically Turkistan, but more particularly the sites at Karakhoja (Kocho) and Murtuk. The harvest was considerable, and immediately Grünwedel planned other missions. In 1904 a second expedition, led by Albert von Le Coq (1860–1930), Grünwedel's collaborator, carried out new excavations at Karakhoja. Manuscripts in various languages were discovered, relating not only to Buddhism but to Nestorianism and Manicheism. The sites at Toyuk and Bezeklik were also visited. Samples of wall paintings were taken from the caves and sent to Berlin, where a good number were de-

2nd and 3rd centuries. He also went to Dunhuang. The existence of the Caves of the Thousand Buddhas, about fifteen kilometres from the town, had been reported by Przhevalsky as well as by Lajos de Loczy, the member of an Austro-Hungarian geological expedition in 1879. At Dunhuang, Stein heard a rumour to the effect that the keeper of the caves, Wang Yuanlu, a Taoist priest, had come across a great number of ancient manuscripts hidden for some time while he had been restoring one of the caves. The discovery had been reported to the authorities in Lanzhou, who had advised silence on the matter. The keeper had set off on a journey when Stein arrived, so he instead turned his attention to what seemed to remain of a section of the Great Wall. He excavated the watch-towers which still existed and found a large number of wooden tablets dating from the Han dynasty. The reading and deciphering of these documents by Chavannes would bring to life the system of frontier patrols compared by Stein, for his part, to the Roman *limes*.

On the return of the keeper, Stein persuaded him to let him examine the hidden manuscripts. Thanks to the mutual respect which Stein and Wang Yuanlu had for the famous pilgrim Xuanzang, Stein managed to gain the keeper's confidence. By way of compensation offered for the reparations made to some caves that the keeper was 'restoring' with an audacity that matched his ignorance, Stein obtained possession of around ten thousand

Left to right: Albert von Le Coq; Albert Grün-wedel; Tachibana Zuicho; Paul Pelliot; Sir Marc Aurel Stein; the forger Islam Akhun.

manuscripts or fragments, mainly in Chinese or Tibetan, as well as paintings on hemp, silk and paper and various objects out of the recess. In the course of this same expedition, Stein also went to Turfan after the German expedition has passed through, and continued towards Karashar, after which he crossed the Takla Makan Desert in the direction of Karadong and Khotan before turning northwards to Aksu and then returning to Khotan. This long and complex journey nearly ended in tragedy, for Stein's right foot was frost-bitten and gangrene threatened. He was therefore evacuated as an emergency case to Leh, in Ladak, where some of his toes were amputated.

At approximately the same time the expedition of Paul Pelliot (1878 – 1945), the only Sinologist to lead a mission, was organised. The French had made a late start. But in 1905, on the initiative of Emile Sénart, an expedition was planned and entrusted to Pelliot, then Professor of Chinese at the French School of Far Eastern Studies at Hanoi. He set off in 1906 in the company of Dr Vaillant, a geographer, and Charles Nouette, a naturalist and photographer. Pelliot first excavated at Tumshuk, then in the region of Kucha, and also at Duldur-Akur and Subashi. When staying subsequently at Urumqi, he was lucky enough to be offered a manuscript from the Dunhuang caves by Duke Lan, a cousin of the emperor who had been exiled to Xinjiang. This confirmed the rumour regarding the discovery of a

cave that was full of them. Pelliot arrived at Dunhuang in February 1908, almost a year after Stein. He stayed there four months, during which time he methodically explored the five hundred odd caves of Mogao. He got Nouette to photograph everything he could, and to copy the inscriptions and the scrolls of the wall paintings. But more than anything, his interest was directed to the manuscripts that had been preserved in their secret hiding-place. He was able to gain access to them and was authorised by Wang Yuanlu to examine everything. He selected everything that seemed to him to be of interest: manuscripts in Chinese and Tibetan, and also in

Sanskrit, Sogdian, Khotanese and Uigur Turkish, dating from the 5th to the 10th century. The recess where they lay had probably been walled up at the beginning of the 11th century, not to be re-opened until nine centuries later. The transaction with Wang was lengthy, but conclusive, and Pelliot was able to take away over six thousand manuscripts, several xylographs, and some paintings. He also obtained a certain number of manuscript and printed fragments in Chinese and Tangut dating from the 13th and 14th centuries from another cave, as well as some Uigur movable type characters. Everything was packed up, loaded, and transported to Peking, then on to France. At Peking, Pelliot showed specimens of his finds to learned Chinese, who urged him to have them copied, photographed and published. The authorities immediately banned any further export of manuscripts.

In 1906, Carl G. Mannerheim, a Finnish colonel in the Russian army, and subsequently President of the Republic of Finland, joined up with Pelliot for a time. The aim of his mission was more military than archaeological. Nevertheless, he brought home from Khotan and Turfan several hundred Chinese and Uigur fragments, which are now preserved in the University Library at Helsinki.

The second expedition organised by Count Ortani was in 1908. Its leader was Tachibana Zuicho. He explored Turfan and Loulan, then Niya and Khotan, while his assistant Nomura Eizaburo excavated at Kucha. But coming soon after the Russo-Japanese War of 1905, he was soon regarded by the Russians, as well as the English, as more of a spy than an archaeologist. In 1908, too, Kozlov, who had already been a member of several expeditions led by Przhevalsky, excavated at Karakhoto, the ruined town of the former kingdom, Xixia, of the Tanguts (1035 – 1368), and brought back a considerable number of manuscripts and printed works dating from this period, in both Chinese and Tangut. Before Kozlov had even returned to St. Petersburg in 1909, another expedition was led by Sergei Oldenburg to Karashar, Kucha and Turfan.

The following year, in 1910, Tachibana returned to Loulan, then made his way to Dunhuang, where Wang Yuanlu let him have about five hundred manuscripts. The order given in Peking did not seem to have been followed, or at any rate was imperfectly followed, and more than ten thousand Chinese manuscripts were taken to Peking, although a certain number slipped through the net and passed to the Japanese expedition as well as to Stein and Oldenburg. The Tibetan manuscripts, however, did not leave the site. The collection that Otani had thus built up would later be dispersed between China (Lüshun, Port Arthur), Korea (Seoul), and Japan (Tyukoku University at Kyoto), with probably a proportion lost.

In 1913, Stein organised a third expedition, financed by the Indian government. He returned to Niya, then excavated at Endere, Miran, Loulan and Dunhuang (where he took several hundred more manuscripts), then in the region of Turfan as well as at Edsengol and Karakhoto, where Kozlov had already excavated. Soon after Stein had been there, Oldenburg obtained at Dunhuang, in 1914, several hundred manuscript scrolls and several thousand fragments from the same cave. In the same period, Le Coq made his fourth German expedition, to both Kucha (Subashi, Kumtura) and Tumshuk,

doing so not without difficulty in view of the delicate situation in Turkistan.

The international situation now put an end to the European archaeological expeditions. And when conditions permitted further ventures, they could only be sucessfully organised under the control of the Chinese. In 1923, when Langdon Warner of the Fogg Art Museum at Harvard wished to make his own attempt, his journey took place under difficult conditions. Moreover, results were unrewarding. At Karakhoto, excavations yielded virtually nothing. At Dunhuang, he discovered that the wall paintings in many caves had been ransacked by White Russians escaping from the USSR. Eventually, he detached a few fragments from the walls and took them back to America. Stein, for his part, had organised another expedition for the benefit of the same museum in 1930. The expedition was short, and the archaeological material, which came mainly from Niya, was abandoned at Kashgar. Stein would die during yet another, final expedition to Afghanistan at the age of 82.

Between 1928 and 1934, Sven Hedin organised another expedition, motorised this time, as a Sino-Swedish under-

taking. The mission ran into trouble as a result of the disturbances then active in Turkistan. Most of the discoveries were taken to Sweden for analysis before being provisionally returned to the Chinese authorities.

At the same time, a motorised Citroën expedition, known as the 'Yellow Crusade', was organised under the leadership of Haardt and Audouin-Dubreuil, with the participation of the palaeontologist Teilhard de Chardin and the archaeologist Joseph Hackin. It has to be said, however, that this was more a motorised trial run than a archaeological expedition.

At the very time when all these expeditions to Turkistan were taking place, Central Asia and most of the staging posts on the old silk routes were also the object of archaeological excavations. But the revival of interest in the Silk Road was no doubt linked more directly to the discoveries made in Turkistan and Central Soviet Asia (Akbeshim near Frunze, Kuva in the Ferghana Valley, Adjina-Tepe in Tadzhikistan, Varakhsa near Bukhara, Pendzhikent near Samarkand, etc.) than to the sites explored in the more westerly areas such as Palmyra of Dura-Europos.

CHRONOLOGY

327 – 325 BC	Alexander the Great in India
c. 165 BC	Yuezhi in Central Asia
139 – 126 BC	Journey of Zhang Qian to Central Asia
104 – 100 BC	Campaigns of Li Guangli in the Ferghana Valley
100 BC	Discovery of the Hippal wind
53 BC	Battle of Carrhae
16 BC	Romans forbidden to wear silk
98	Mission of Gan Ying to the Roman Empire
166	Mission of Antoninus
226	Arrival in China of a merchant from Da Qin
366	Caves of Mogao near Dunhuang begun
4th century	Caves of Binglingsi begun
399 – 414	Journey of Faxian to India
404 – 424	Journey of Shimeng to India
420	Departure of Fayong for India
5th century	Sericulture introduced to Khotan
518 – 522	Journey of Songyun to India
mid-6th century	Sericulture introduced to Constantinople
567	Mission of the Sogdian Maniakh to Constantinople
629 – 645	Journey of Xuanzang to Central Asia and India
635	Arrival in Changan of the Nestorian Aluoben
651	Sassanid prince Peroz takes refuge in China
671 – 695	Journey of Yijing to India by sea
751	Battle of Talas between Chinese and Arabs
751 – 790	Journey of Wukong to India
755	Revolt of An Lushan, Chinese general of Central Asian origin
781	Nestorian stele of Xian
c. 815	Journey of Ibn Wahab to China
845	Proscription of foreign religions in China
981 – 983	Mission of Wang Yande to Gaochang
1221 – 1224	Journey of Chang Chun to the region of Samarkand
1245 – 1247	Journey of Joannes de Plano Carpini to Asia
1249 – 1251	Journey of André de Longjumeau to Asia
1253 – 1255	Journey of William of Ruysbroeck to Asia
1259	Mission of Chang De to Baghdad
1261 – 1265	Journey of Matteo and Niccolò Polo to Asia
1271 – 1295	Journey of Marco Polo to Asia
1278	Departure of Rabban bar Sauma and Marqus for the West
1287	Arrival of Rabban bar Sauma in Paris
1289	Departure of Jean de Montcorvin for China
1315 – 1330	Journey of Odoric de Pordenone to Asia
1340	Pegolotti's *La Pratica della mercatura*
1396 – 1415	Mission of Chen Cheng to Herat
1419 – 1423	Mission of Ghiyath ed-Din to China
c. 1500	Stay of Sayyid Ali Khitayi in China
1603 – 1605	Journey of Beneditto Goës from India to China
1877	Invention of the name 'Silk Road'
1890	First archaeological expeditions to Central Asia

BIBLIOGRAPHY

Along the ancient Silk Routes: Central Asian Art from the West Berlin State Museum, New York, 1982.

Andrews, F. H., 'Ancient Chinese figured silk excavated', in *The Burlington Magazine,* July – September, 1920.

Belenitsky, Alexandr, *The Ancient Civilization of Central Asia* (trans. J. Hogarth), London, 1969.

Barthold, W., *Histoire des Turcs d'Asie centrale,* Paris, 1945.

Boulnois, Luce, *La Route de Soie,* Paris, 1963.

Bréhier, Louis, *La civilisation byzantine,* Paris, 1950.

Bretschneider, E., *Mediaeval Researches from Eastern Asiatic Sources,* 2 vols, London, 1988.

Bussagli, Mario, *La Peinture de l'Asie centrale,* Geneva, 1963.

Chavannes, Edouard, *Dix inscriptions chinoises de l'Asie centrale,* Paris 1902.

– , *Les documents chinois découverts par Aurel Stein dans les sables du Turkestan oriental,* Oxford, 1913.

– , *Documents sur les Tout-kiue (Turcs) occidentaux,* Paris, n. d.

– , (trans.), *Les mémoires historiques de Se-ma Ts'ien,* 6 vols, Paris, 1895 – 1969.

– , 'Les pays d'Occident d'après le Heou Han chou', in *T'oung Pao,* 8 (1907).

– , 'Les pays d'Occident d'après le Wei-lio', in *T'oung Pao,* 6 (1905).

– , 'Trois généraux chinois de la dynastie des Han orientaux', in *T'oung Pao,* 7 (1906).

– , 'Voyage de Song-yun dans l'Udanyâna et le Gandhâra', in *Bulletin de l'Ecole française d'Extrême-Orient,* 3 (1903).

Christensen, A., *L'Iran sous les Sassanides,* Copenhagen, 1944.

Coedes, Georges, *Textes d'auteurs grecs et latins relatifs à l'Extrême-Orient,* Paris, 1910.

Dabbs, Jack, *History of the Discovery and Exploration of Chinese Turkestan,* The Hague, 1963.

Dubs, Homer H., *A Roman City in Ancient China,* London, 1957.

– , (trans.), *History of the Former Han Dynasty,* 3 vols, Baltimore, 1938 – 1955.

Dutreuil de Rhins, J.L. and Grenard, F., *Mission scientifique dans la Haute-Asie,* 3 vols, Paris, 1897.

Emmerick, R.E., *Tibetan Texts Concerning Khotan,* London, 1967.

Enoki, Kazuo, 'The location of the capital Lou-lan and the date of the Karosthi documents', in *Memoirs of the Research Department of the Toyo Bunko,* 22 (1963).

– , *Shiruku rodo no rekishi kara* (On the history of the Silk Road), Tokyo, 1979.

Evans, E., *Francesco Balduccio Pegolotti. La pratica della mercatura,* Cambridge (Mass.), 1936.

Fauvel, Albert, *Les séricigènes sauvages de la Chine,* Paris, 1895.

Ferrand, Gabriel, *Relations de voyages et textes géographiques arabes, persans et turcs relatifs à l'Extrême-Orient du VIIIe au XVIIIe siècle,* 2 vols, Paris, 1913 – 1914.

Filliozat, Jean, *Les relations extérieures de l'Inde,* Pondicherry, 1956.

Foucher, Alfred, *L'art gréco-bouddhique du Gandhâra,* 3 vols, Paris-Hanoi, 1905 – 1922.

– , *La vieille route de l'Inde de Bactres à Taxila,* Paris, 1942.

Frumkin, Gregory, *Archeology in Soviet Central Asia,* Leiden, 1970.

Gernet, Jacques, 'Location de chameaux pour des voyages, à Touen-houang', in *Mélanges de sinologies offerts à M. Paul Demiéville,* I, Paris, 1966.

Ghirshman, Roman, *Bergram. Recherches archéologiques et historiques sur les kouchans,* Cairo, 1946.

– , *Parthes et Sassanides,* Paris, 1962.

Grenet, Frantz, *Les pratiques funéraires dans l'Asie centrale sédentaire de la conquête grecque à l'islamisation,* Paris, 1984.

Hackin, Joseph, Godard, A. and Y., *Les antiquités bouddhiques de Bamiyan,* 2 vols, Paris, 1928.

Hambis, Louis (ed.), *L'Asie centrale,* Paris, 1977.

– , *Mission Paul Pelliot,* various dates.

Haneda, Akira, *Saiiki* (The Regions of the West), Tokyo, 1969.

Harada, Yoshito, 'The interchange of Eastern and Western cultures as evidenced in the Shôsô-in Treasures', in *Memoirs of the Research Department of the Toyo Bunko,* 11 (1939).

Harmatta, J. (ed.), *Prolegomena to the sources on the history of pre-islamic Central Asia,* Budapest, 1979.

Haussig, H.W., *Die Geschichte Zentralasiens und der Seidenstrasse,* Darmstadt, 1983.

Hayashi, Ryoichi, *The Silk Road and the Shoso-in,* Tokyo-New York, 1975.

Hedin, Sven, *History of the Expedition in Asia, 1927 – 1935,* Stockholm 1943 – 1944.

Herrmann, Albert, *Die alten Seidenstrassen zwischen China and Syrien,* n. p., 1910.

– , *Loulan: China, Indien and Rom im Lichte der Ausgrabungen am Lobnor,* Leipzig, 1931.

Hirth, F., *China and the Roman Orient,* Leipzig-Shanghai, 1885.

Hopkirk, Peter, *Foreign Devils on the Silk Road,* London, 1980.

Hoyanagi, Mutsumi, 'Natural changes of the region along the Old Silk Road in the Tarim Basin in historical times', in *Memoirs of the Research Department of the Toyo Bunko,* 33 (1975).

Hudson, G.F., *Europe and China,* London, 1931.

Hulsewe, A.F.P., 'Quelques considérations sur le commerce de la soie au temps de la dynastie des Han', in *Mélanges de sinologie offerts à M. Paul Demiéville,* II, Paris, 1974.

Hulsewe, A.F.P., Loewe, M.A.N., *China in Central Asia: the early stage, 125* BC – AD *123,* Leiden, 1979.

Ibn Battuta, *Voyages* (trans. C. Defremy and B.R. Sanguinetti), 3 vols, Paris, 1982.

Ingolt, Harald, *Gandharan Art in Pakistan,* Hamden (Ct.), 1971.

Ishida, Mikinosuke, *Toyo bunkashi soko* (Studies in the Cultural History of Eastern Asia), Tokyo, 1973.

Julien, Stanislas (trans.), *Hiouen-thsang. Memoires sur les contrées occidentales,* 2 vols, Paris, 1867.

– , (trans.), *Histoire de la vie de Hiouen-thsang,* Paris, 1853.

– , *Mélanges de géographie asiatique et de philologie sinico-indienne,* Paris, 1864.

– , *Résumé des principaux traités chinois sur la culture du mûrier et l'éducation des vers à soie,* Paris, 1837.

Kuhn, Dieter, 'Silk technology in the Sung period (960–1278)', in *T'oung Pao,* 67 (1981).

–, 'The silk-workshops of the Shang dynasty (16th–11th century BC), in *Explorations in the History of Science and Technology in China, compiled in honour of the eightieth birthday of Dr. Joseph Needham,* Shanghai, 1982.

Laufer, Berthold, *Sino-iranica,* Chicago, 1919.

Le Coq, Albert von, *Chotscho,* Berlin, 1913.

Le Fèvre, Georges, *La croisière jaune,* Paris, 1933.

Liu, Mau-tsai, *Kutscha und seine Beziehungen zu China zum 2. Jh. v. Chr. bis zum 6. Jh. n. Chr.,* Göttingen, 1969.

Magnin, Paul, 'Le pèlerinage dans la tradition bouddhique chinoise', in *Les pèlerinages dans les régions non-chrétiennes,* Paris, 1986.

Mahler, Jane Gaston, *The Westerners among the Figurines of the T'ang Dynasty of China,* Rome, 1959.

Maillard, Monique, 'Essai sur la vie matérielle dans l'oasis de Turfan pendant le Haut Moyen-Age', in *Arts asiatiques,* 29 (1973).

–, *Grottes et monuments d'Asie centrale,* Paris, 1983.

Mannerheim, C.G., *Across Asia from West to East,* 2 vols, Helsinki, 1940.

–, 'Manuscrits et inscriptions de Haute-Asie du Ve au XIe siècle', in *Journal asiatique,* 269 (1981).

Maspero, Henri, *Les documents chinois de la troisième expédition de Sir Aurel Stein en Asie centrale,* London, 1953.

–, 'Un texte inconnu sur le pays de Ta-ts'in (Orient romain)', in *Mélanges Maspero,* II, Cairo, 1937.

Mazaheri, Aly, *La Route de la Soie,* Paris, 1983.

Moule, A.C., *Christians in China Before the Year 1550,* London, 1930.

NHK (ed.), *Shiruku rodo* (The Silk Road), 12 vols, Tokyo, 1980–1984.

Pariset, Ernest, *Histoire de la soie,* Lyon, 1843.

Pelliot, Paul, 'Deux itinéraires de Chine en Inde à la fin du VIIIe siècle', in *Bulletin de l'Ecole française d'Extrême-Orient,* 4 (1904).

–, 'Les influences iraniennes en Asie centrale et en Extrême-Orient', in *Revue d'histoire et de littérature religieuses* (1911).

–, *Notes on Marco Polo,* 2 vols, Paris, 1959–1963.

–, *Recherches sur les chrétiens d'Asie centrale et d'Extrême-Orient,* 2 vols, Paris, 1973–1984.

–, 'Une bibliothèque mediévale retrouvée au Kan-sou', in *Bulletin de l'Ecole française d'Extrême-Orient,* 8 (1908).

Petech, Luciano, 'La description des pays d'Occident de Che Tao-ngan', in *Mélanges de sinologie offerts à M. Paul De-*

miéville, I (1966).

–, 'Les marchands italiens dans l'empire mongol', in *Journal asiatique,* 250 (1962).

Pfister, R., 'Les soieries Han de Palmyre', in *Revue des arts asiatiques,* 13, 2 (1937).

–, *Textiles de Palmyre,* Paris, 1934.

–, *Nouveaux textiles de Palmyre,* Paris, 1937.

–, *Textiles de Palmyre,* III, Paris, 1940.

Plan Carpin, Jean du, *Histoire des Mongols* (trans. L.C. Schmitt), Paris, 1961.

Pline l'Ancien, *Histoire naturelle* (var. trans.), coll. G. Budé, var. dates.

Polo, Marco, *La Description du Monde* (ed. L. Hambis), Paris, 1955.

Pulleyblank, E.G., 'A Sogdian colony in Inner Mongolia', in *T'oung Pao,* 41 (1952).

Reinaud, M., *Relations politiques et commerciales de l'empire romain avec l'Asie orientale,* Paris, 1863.

Remusat, Abel, *Histoire de la ville de Khotan,* Paris, 1820.

–, (trans.), *Foe koue ki ou Relation des royaumes bouddhiques,* Paris, 1836.

Riboud, Krishna and Luobo-Lesnichenko, E., 'Nouvelles découvertes soviétiques à Oglakty et leur analogie avec les soies façonnées polychromes de Leou-lan, dynastie des Han', in *Arts asiatiques,* 28 (1973).

–, and Vial, Gabriel, 'Les soieries Han', in *Arts asiatiques,* 17 (1968).

Ricci, Matthieu and Trigault, Nicolas, *Histoire de l'expédition chrétienne au royaume de la Chine (1581–1610),* Paris, 1978.

Richthofen, F. von, *China,* Berlin, 1877.

Rostovtzeff, M., *Dura-Europos and its Art,* Oxford, 1938.

Rubrouck, Guillaume de, *Voyage dans l'empire mongol,* Paris, 1985.

Rudenko, Sergei, *Frozen Tombs of Siberia: the Pazyryk Burials of Iron-Age Horsemen,* London, 1970.

–, *Die Kultur der Hsiung-nu und die Hügelgräber von Noin-Ula,* Bonn, 1969.

Saeki, P.Y., *The Nestorian Documents and Relics in China,* Tokyo, 1937.

Schafer, Edward H., 'The camel in China down to the Mongol dynasty', in *Sinologica,* 2 (1950).

–, *The Golden Peaches of Samarkand,* Berkeley-Los Angeles, 1963.

Schoff, W.H., *The Periplus of the Erythrean Sea,* New York, 1912.

Shiratori, Kurakichi, Special number of the *Memoirs of the Research Department of the Toyo Bunko,* 15 (1956).

Sinor, Denis, *Introduction à l'étude de l'Eurasie centrale,* Wiesbaden, 1963.

Soymie, Michel (ed.), *Les peintures murales et les manuscrits de Dunhuang,* Paris, 1984.

Starcky, J., *Palmyre,* Paris, 1952.

Stein, Aurel, *Ancient Khotan,* 2 vols, Oxford, 1907.

–, *Innermost Asia,* Oxford, 1928.

–, *On Ancient Central Asian Tracks,* London, 1933.

–, *Ruins of Desert Cathay,* London, 1912.

–, *Serindia,* Oxford, 1921.

Sylwan, Vivi, *Investigation of Silk from Edsengol and Lop-nor,* Stockholm, 1949.

–, 'Silk from the Yin dynasty', in *Bulletin of the Museum of Far Eastern Antiquities,* 9 (1937).

Tavernier, Jean-Baptiste, *Les six voyages en Turquie et en Perse,* 2 vols, Paris, 1981.

Tarzi, Zemaryalai, *L'architecture et le décor rupestre des grottes de Bâmiyân,* 2 vols, Paris, 1977.

Thévenot, Jean, *Voyage du Levant,* Paris, 1980.

Tonko bakkikutsu (The caves of Mogao at Dunhuang), 5 vols, Tokyo, 1980–1982.

Waldschmidt, E., *Gandhara, Kutscha, Turfan,* Leipzig, 1925.

Warner, Langdon, *The Long Old Road to China,* New York, 1926.

Whitfield, Roderick, *The Art of Central Asia: The Stein Collection of the British Museum,* 3 vols, Tokyo, 1982–1984.

Willets, William, *L'art de la Chine,* Lausanne, 1968.

Xia, Nai, *Kaoguxue de kejishi* (Essays on the archaeology of science and technology in China), Beijing, 1979.

Xiang, Da, *Tangdai Chang'an yu Xiyu wenming* (Chang'an and the culture of the regions of the West under the Tang dynasty), Beijing, 1957.

Yü, Ying-shih, *Trade and Expansion in Han China,* Berkeley-Los Angeles, 1967.

Yule, Sir Henry, *Cathay and the Way Thither,* rev. Henri Cordier, 4 vols, London, 1915.

Zürcher, Erik, *The Buddhist Conquest of China,* 2 vols, Leiden, 1959.

PICTURE CREDITS